A Place Where Everybody Matters

The House of Prisca and Aquila

OUR MISSION AT THE HOUSE OF PRISCA AND AQUILA IS TO PRODUCE QUAL-ITY books that expound accurately the word of God to empower women and men to minister together in a multicultural church. Our writers have a positive view of the Bible as God's revelation that affects both thoughts and words, so it is plenary, historically accurate, and consistent in itself; fully reliable; and authoritative as God's revelation. Because God is true, God's revelation is true, inclusive to men and women and speaking to a multicultural church, wherein all the diversity of the church is represented within the parameters of egalitarianism and inerrancy.

The word of God is what we are expounding, thereby empowering women and men to minister together in all levels of the church and home. The reason we say women and men together is because that is the model of Prisca and Aquila, ministering together to another member of the church—Apollos: "Having heard Apollos, Priscilla and Aquila took him aside and more accurately expounded to him the Way of God" (Acts 18:26). True exposition, like true religion, is by no means boring—it is fascinating. Books that reveal and expound God's true nature "burn within us" as they elucidate the Scripture and apply it to our lives.

This was the experience of the disciples who heard Jesus on the road to Emmaus: "Were not our hearts burning while Jesus was talking to us on the road, while he was opening the scriptures to us?" (Luke 24:32). We are hoping to create the classics of tomorrow: significant and accessible trade and academic books that "burn within us."

Our "house" is like the home to which Prisca and Aquila no doubt brought Apollos as they took him aside. It is like the home in Emmaus where Jesus stopped to break bread and reveal his presence. It is like the house built on the rock of obedience to Jesus (Matt 7:24). Our "house," as a euphemism for our publishing team, is a home where truth is shared and Jesus' Spirit breaks bread with us, nourishing all of us with his bounty of truth.

We are delighted to work together with Wipf and Stock in this series and welcome submissions on a variety of topics from an egalitarian inerrantist global perspective. The House of Prisca and Aquila is also a ministry center affiliated with the International Council of Community Churches.

For more information visit www.houseofpricsaandaquila.com.

A Place Where Everybody Matters

Life and Ministry in a Small Church

JEAN F. RISLEY

WIPF & STOCK · Eugene, Oregon

A PLACE WHERE EVERYBODY MATTERS
Life and Ministry in a Small Church

House of Prisca and Aquila Series

www.wipfandstock.com

ISBN 13: 978-1-60899-306-2

Manufactured in the U.S.A.

This book is dedicated to the Holy Spirit, whose living presence is very real within and among the people of the Scotchtown Presbyterian Church.

Contents

Preface

A Place Where Everybody Matters is a gem of a book; it sparkles with fresh enthusiasm as it communicates what a grand privilege and honor it is before our Lord to either pastor or lead a small church. Oftentimes, small church pastors or leaders become deeply discouraged as they try to balance the multiplicity of ministry and administrative tasks that they do from day to day with such little resources that they often feel overwhelmed and inadequate, leading to feelings of failure. Now add to that the ongoing negative messages that the small church and it's pastor/leader are bombarded with such as "bigger is better," or "grow your church from the outside in," or "get bigger and lead your church to grow explosively" and it is no wonder that the turnover rate for small church pastors/leaders is so high. What pastors and leaders of a small church need is encouragement and a greater understanding of their role before God. And this is precisely what *A Place Where Everybody Matters* will do for you, for it did it for me!

After having read this well-planned, Spirit inspired book, I felt infused with encouragement and have never felt more thrilled about the opportunity that God has given me to pastor my small church. And I think what made the big difference is that while I was reading *A Place Where Everybody Matters* I felt that the author "had been there and done that" and I could resonate strongly with much of what she learned and understood from pastoring her own small church. Her personal expertise not only as a former small church pastor but also as a former business manager enabled her to examine the organizational model of the small church from perspectives that I had never thought about before, and this insight helped tremendously.

She understands the function of the small church well and is able to see it from three different aspects (or parts): 1) the small church environment, the reality of what life is like in a small church as it seeks to place Jesus Christ at the front and center of its ministry, 2) the work and activities of a small church, where everyone—men, women, and children participate together in God's handiwork, feeling a sense of purpose and belonging as they seek to further God's kingdom and 3) the pastoral role of the small church, bringing a deeper understanding of how life is different for a pastor and the people of a small church in comparison to larger churches, and how the expectations of each, pastor and the body, needs to be adjusted in order for the church to grow and thrive according to God's ordained plan.

As a pastor of a small church myself for nearly a decade, I love the insight and revelation that the author brings to her work, that can not help but strongly encourage and support small church pastors and leaders so much so that they will actually enjoy God and the work God has appointed them to do. This way of thinking lets us relax into our calling, realizing that the small church is intentionally a place where the whole family of God, not just the pastor/leader, uses all their gifts and works together to fulfill the great commission. The small church, when it functions the way God originally intended, is God's creative and loving way of giving us a little taste of heaven on earth—truly a place where everybody matters.

Rev. Dr. Leslie McKinney,
New Year's Day, 2010
Pastor of Pilgrim Church, Beverly, Massachusetts
author of *Accepted in the Beloved: A Devotional Bible Study For Women on Finding Healing and Wholeness in God's Love* (2008 Wipf and Stock, House of Prisca and Aquila Series)

PART I

The Small-Church Environment

Introduction

ARE YOU A PASTOR or a leader or a participant in a small church? Have you even been embarrassed about the size of your church? When you tell someone who asks how many people come to your church, do they look at you with pity or concern? Do folks tell you about how much bigger their churches are or how fast they are growing? Does it feel like people think that your small church is somehow not good enough because it is just not big enough?

Malarkey, balderdash, and other less polite words! Paul's churches in the New Testament were probably not much bigger than yours, and maybe even smaller—and they changed the entire western world! God has been at work in and through the people of small churches from that time to this, in every era of history. You should never need to be embarrassed about the size of your church, and by the time you finish this book you will know why small churches are such good places to grow in faith and to live out our lives as disciples of Jesus.

A small church is a place where everybody matters. Every contribution is needed, and each person can see the way his or her own work contributes to the work of the church. There is always more work that needs to be done than there are people to do it, so each person who does his or her part of the work is visibly valuable. We all work together, teaching each other and learning from each other as we go, and so growing in faith is something that each person is busy both doing and encouraging in others.

Some churches are in denial about their smallness, still living and spending money as if they were bigger churches. Some small churches still hope to be rescued from their smallness by a change in the economy, new people moving into the area, or a new pastor. When the people of a small church realize that size and money are not going to be available to "fix" their "problems," the door is open for them to truly become the church themselves. They can see that the church will not do anything that they do not do themselves and that the church will not be anything that they do not make happen. When the people take ownership of doing the work of the church, they become the active representatives of Christ in their own neighborhood.

In this way, being part of a small church can be an unparalleled opportunity to live as a member of the body of Christ. No one is in the audience. Everyone is an active participant. Everybody has a contribution to make, and everybody's contribution matters.

WHAT IS A SMALL CHURCH?

What does it mean to be a small church? One of my favorite definitions comes from Richard H. Bliese in *Christian Century*:

> A small church can be defined as one in which the number of active members and the total annual budget are inadequate relative to organizational needs and expenses. It is a church struggling to pay its minister, heat its building, and find enough people to assume leadership responsibilities.[1]

Do you see yourself and your church in this definition? I know that we did, and many other churches, both bigger and smaller, probably do too.

The church where I found myself is one that struggles to find the resources, both people and money, to do the ministry it feels called to do. In fact, this church has been struggling for so long, for almost all of its two-hundred-year history, that the struggle has become the normal state. The brief times in history when the church was "comfortable," those periods of regional growth in the 1840s and the 1970s, are times we always look to as golden memories. The reality is that, for most of the years between the first meeting of neighbors in the house across the street in 1796 and next Sunday's worship service, almost everything the church has done has been a stretch.

This church is not alone. Most experts consider a church to be small when it has fewer than 200 members or has fewer than 150 people in worship on an ordinary Sunday. From our perspective, and maybe from yours, even those levels of membership and attendance can seem heavenly, because our membership and attendance are usually less than half of those minimum numbers.

---

1. Bliese, "Life," 24.

WE HAVE A LOT OF COMPANY IN OUR SMALLNESS.

These days, many of the churches in our mainline Protestant denominations are small, and the number of small churches is growing. For my denomination, the Presbyterian Church (USA), the number of churches with fewer than one hundred members is consistently increasing, while the numbers of churches in the larger size categories is consistently decreasing. As you can see in the following table, both in our region and nationally, there are more smaller churches and fewer larger churches over an eight-year period:[2]

Churches by Number of Members	1999	2007	GAIN/LOSS
Northeast Region			
churches with 1–50	173	259	+50%
churches with 51–100	247	266	+8%
churches with 101–200	362	328	-9%
churches more than 200	397	307	-27%
National Totals			
churches with 1–50	2,497	2,845	+14%
churches with 51–100	2,326	2,451	+5%
churches with 101–200	2,655	2,437	-8%
churches more than 200	3,717	3,059	-18%

This Presbyterian experience is not unique, and many other denominations share this trend. We have a growing number of small churches, and many churches that have not been small need to come to terms with their new life as small churches.

You may have experienced some of the reasons for this increasing number of small churches. An overall decline in membership across the mainline denominations is felt in individual churches as a decline in size. This comes as a result of many factors: an increase in very large churches, often outside the traditional denominations; more alternative forms of worship; transportation making many more worship choices accessible; modern expectation that the worship experience compete with movies

---

2. PC (USA) Research Services *Comparative Statistics*, 6, 30.

and television; and use of traditional Sunday morning worship time for secular activities like sports and shopping.

The result is that many churches that had not thought of themselves as small churches are becoming small. Since this is a kind of bad news, we tend to avoid thinking about it, hoping that, if we just hold out a little longer, things will turn around. Denial can lead us to using resources we don't have to support ministry patterns that no longer work for our actual church size. Focusing on the fact that things aren't the way they used to be can get in the way of figuring out how to do effective ministry as the small churches we are now.

However our small church came to be small—whether it's just starting out, has been small for generations, or has just found itself in a newer, smaller size—it still has a call to ministry in Christ, and it does have a lot of company in its smallness.

SHOULD WE BE TRYING TO BE A BIGGER CHURCH?

Our church is not a rapidly growing church, and yours probably isn't either. With the exception of a few hectic periods in the church's life, the attendance on Sunday mornings has been pretty much the same for two centuries. When we look at books about small churches, it seems that the main goal most experts have for a small church is to stop being a small church and become something bigger.

Growth does sound like a good thing, a sign that we're doing something right. Many small churches have been seduced into following the holy grail of growth, looking for the numbers that would somehow prove that their ministry was "successful."

There are lots of arguments about why bigger is better. With more money, a church can afford more and higher quality programs, better materials, more skilled and experienced staff, and more comfortable and presentable facilities. More people mean that there are groups of people, and not just a few individuals, in each of the age groups and interest categories, like young families or older singles. This makes it possible to offer more programs for specific needs.

The economics of scale are real. If a church has 150 or more people in worship each week, there is probably enough money not only to pay for a full-time pastor, but also to hire other supporting staff. There are likely enough qualified program leaders, with professional support, to offer programs with the quality that modern entertainment has led people to expect. There are enough people to put together social service projects or mission teams without taking time or resources from other critical areas of the church.

Since most of the challenges in a small church seem to depend on limited resources, it's hard not to think that our size is the cause of our problems. After all, if we were only a little bigger and had a little more money, today's top three problems could be solved. What we don't realize is that our expectations grow with our available resources, and that the problems to be solved don't go away. More importantly, big changes in size lead to a completely different set of problems that result from changes in scale for the things we were already doing well.

Should we be trying to be a bigger church? I believe that the answer to this question is not obvious. If we spend our time focusing on how we can grow our church, we waste a lot of the energy and attention that we need to give to *being* the church in this present moment. If we do a good job of the ministry that's put into our hands, growth may or may not follow, depending on many factors outside of our control.

Rapid growth may come to a particular church at a particular time, when its ministry to the population it serves is effective and when the population it serves is growing rapidly. This time of growth can be a very great blessing to all of the people involved. It is a result of a church finding and following its ministry opportunity faithfully, and it is one more reason to give thanks to God. But for each particular church, the challenge is not to find the magic formula that will lead to growth, but to find the ministry and community it is called to serve.

THE BIG QUESTION: WHY ARE WE HERE?

Why are we here? What are our churches here to do? Small churches, like our larger counterparts, are here to follow the instructions Jesus gave in the Great Commission, to make disciples. He said,

> make disciples of all nations, baptizing them in the name of the Father and of the Son and of the Holy Spirit, and teaching them to obey everything that I have commanded you. (Matt 28:19–20)

A small church is a great place to become a disciple: a great place to learn from those who have gone before us and a place to teach those who are coming after us.

Why are we here? Our treasurer always has a quick answer to this question: "to keep the doors open." This may sound like a strategy of survival at all costs, of holding onto the past even when all that the church used to do and be is fading away. You may know what it feels like to struggle to be able to do as much as you did last year. But being a church is much more than just the struggle to keep going.

For us, keeping the doors open means not just to keep the building open and the lights on, but to keep the gospel of Jesus Christ available to any people who need to hear it, whether they are completely new to it or have followed Jesus all their lives. In the process, we encourage each other to grow in faith, support each other in need or crisis, and continue the work that Jesus began in the world.

What is this work? It is the work of becoming disciples of Jesus Christ. It begins when a person is drawn to learn about him and listen to him. It becomes central when a person accepts Jesus as the primary authority in life and enters into a personal relationship with him. It continues as a lifelong process of learning, growing, and working to do all that Jesus commands. The church is here to help in each stage of this process of developing discipleship, for every person who comes to us, at whatever stage in the process they find themselves.

Can we do it? We've managed so far, and with God's help we'll make it another year or two. Every year, even the leanest and most difficult, has seen this church on this corner as a witness to God's presence in the world. For us, this is our achievement. We witness to and serve the people of the community where we find ourselves, and we support the others who are called to do this work in other parts of the world. We hope to continue this work as long as it's possible for us, no matter how pessimistic the experts might become about the viability of small churches like us.

HOW DO WE DO MINISTRY AS A SMALL CHURCH?

The purpose of this book is to look at the ministry of small churches based on practical experience and to explore what things seem to work in a small church. We'll look at the environment, culture, and activities in the small church and then think about the kind of pastoral role best suited to helping a small church thrive. We'll also look at the small church from the pastor's side, considering what the work of ministry looks like in a small church and what kind of pastor will be able to serve effectively there.

Introduction

My goal in writing is to share some of what I've learned and been taught by the people of the Scotchtown Presbyterian Church. I hope that you can find suggestions and examples to help you in your own ministry, whether you're a participant in a small church, a pastor, or an administrator responsible for small churches. If our small churches are to rediscover the joy of following Jesus Christ, they need to regain their respect for their own ministry and to value their particular and unique divine calling.

I hope you'll find that, by understanding better how our small churches work, you'll appreciate them more and come to enjoy being part of the work of Jesus in and through a small church.

QUESTIONS FOR REFLECTION AND DISCUSSION

1. Have you participated in a small church? Have you been a leader or a pastor in a small church?

2. What are the struggles that your small church has faced?

3. What are your church's strengths? What are its weaknesses?

4. How do you follow the teaching and example of Jesus in your church?

5. How do you live out the Great Commission in your church?

2

What Life Is Like in the Small Church

WE ALL KNOW EACH OTHER VERY, VERY WELL.

A SMALL CHURCH IS a place where almost everybody knows almost everybody else. There are few enough of us in worship that it's possible to greet and talk to most of the people there, either before worship or at the coffee hour afterward. If your church, like ours, has a time to greet each other with peace, you're probably able to shake hands or share a hug with most everyone in the room.

Folks in our church pretty much sit in the same places week after week. I used to joke that, as a pastor, I could take attendance the way they did long ago in schools: by marking which spaces were empty. Dianne, a gifted nurse with a twinkling sense of humor, once convinced the friends she sat with to test me on that. They decided to move forward one pew each week to see how long it would take me to notice. It took three weeks before it was obvious that they had moved to a different "neighborhood," and another week before I got the courage to ask them what was going on. In your own church, you can probably point out each of the areas where the different families gather.

Everyone notices a new face in our church, and words of welcome come to a stranger from all different directions. We do try to strike a balance, to be welcoming without being too overwhelming to our visitors. Visitors can feel both ways about us, wanting to be noticed but not wanting to be the victim of a sales blitz. It's important for small-church folks not to get into the rut of talking only to the same people every week. We even try to ask those who stay with us for a while what made them feel welcome at first, so that we can get better at making people feel comfortable.

Each small church draws people from the surrounding community, and so the degree of change in the congregation reflects the mobility of the families that live nearby. In our church, some of the families who were part of the founding two hundred years ago are still active. Many who move out of the neighborhood, but stay in the area, drive by several other churches to come to their "home" church.

The people of a small church have a lot of history together. Two women whose grandchildren are grown up remember that they became friends when they met in the communicants class as teenagers. Two teenage girls, who may have very little in common on the surface, have simply known each other all their lives, since they came through Sunday School, Christmas pageants, Easter egg hunts, youth projects, and Vacation Bible School together. Shared experiences make for bonds that change in intensity at different stages of life, but are always part of the undercurrent of our relationships.

We remember the major transitions and events of each other's lives—the baptisms, the major illnesses, the miscarriages, the times of joining the church, the marriages, and the family funerals. We have celebrated together when things go well—the long anniversaries, the graduations, the special awards, the new jobs, and the times we were in the right place at the right time. We have been there for each other when the jobs were lost, accidents left us disabled, relationships were troubled, or mental illness struck those we love.

We know what each other is like—who likes to gossip, who can keep a confidence, who can be depended on for a casserole in a crisis, who to call for comfort, and who to call for a challenge or to build up your courage. We know each other's weaknesses—who's winning their battle with alcohol, who slid off the wagon, whose temper made for trouble on the job, who's struggling to make ends meet, and whose credit card is out of control. We know who we can trust and which things different folks can be trusted to be and do.

We talk to each other a lot, and the grapevine is alive and well. One parishioner joked that "there are three ways to spread the news: telephone, telegraph, and tell Karen." I can think of at least a dozen names that could be substituted for Karen's in that sentence. Instant messaging among the young people and email and cell phones for everyone have only increased the speed and reliability of communications. The word of a concern, a need, or a death spreads through the community very quickly.

Questions, concerns, new ideas, and possible changes also pass through the informal communication channels. Whatever the issue, whether it's to use prisoners from the local jail to do some painting or taking on a mission appeal for Christmas, the informal communication channels inform our decisions. When did we do it before? Who was involved? How did it turn out? Is there somebody with the time and interest to take care of it? When a topic has filtered through those who care about it, then our pooled experience is engaged, folks have time to think and pray about it, and a sense of the community emerges. When it becomes time to make a formal commitment, the whys and hows and whos of a particular activity usually have been thought through pretty thoroughly.

WE ARE FAMILY, AND YOU CAN'T CHOOSE YOUR RELATIVES.

The people of a small church relate together as a family. At least in part because of our smallness, a higher percentage of our congregation is actually related to each other than would be true in a larger church. But within the church community, people actually do relate to each other as an extended family.

As in families by blood, members of the church family may not have much in common with each other, other that the common bond of being in the same family. We are multigenerational, from the youngest children to those with grown grandchildren. We have all different interests (from flower arranging to science fiction), all different levels of education (from not finishing high school to graduate degrees), and all different kinds of work (including unskilled labor, skilled trades, law enforcement, and medical professionals). Some are in school, some are working, some are homemakers, some are volunteers, and some are retired. We are married, single, widowed, and divorced. Some are parents and some have been childless. Some have just come to this country, while others have been here for generations.

We are family because we are all adopted into the family of God through Jesus Christ. When we accept Jesus as our Lord, all of the others who also accept him become our brothers and sisters. This is not negotiable. We receive this family with our faith. The starting point of our church family is that it is built on our faith, not our similarities, our compatibility, or even our feelings for each other. We simply are connected. Just like the families we're born into, we can't choose our relatives in church, either. We belong to our relatives in the church family whether we feel like it or not, whether we like it or not. We don't choose our relatives in Christ, and we can't get rid of them either. We simply have to learn to live together.

The family of the brothers and sisters of Jesus is not a closed circle. All are welcome into God's family, and it's important, especially in the small church, to remember that all are welcome in our little corner of it. We're charged to welcome all who come to us, and, in obedience to the Great Commission, we're charged to invite everyone in that we can. Being welcoming to all is a requirement for the church, and offering sincere invitations to all is part of our commitment to evangelism.

All people who are part of the church family, whether for a short or long time, have one thing in common beside our commitment to Christ: We all acknowledge that we are sinful people. We're not perfect, and the better we come to know Jesus, the more we appreciate our own failings. It's critically important that we accept each other as family members as we are, including our sinfulness and failings as well as our best behavior and Sunday clothes. We can't disconnect from a natural cousin simply because they're rude, crude, or fresh out of prison, and the same is true for our fellow members of the family in the church.

WE HAVE A LOT OF HISTORY TOGETHER.

Because the people of the small church have typically been together for many years, we have a lot of history together. We remember the accidents in space, assassinations, and terrorist attacks that we all experienced together. We were upset by the same news of government corruption, sexual misconduct, and tragic accidents. We have our local view of what's important in the wider world, and we're all touched by the local events that affect our family members.

Over the years, we've developed our own traditions, trying new things once in a while, and incorporating the things that worked into our habits. Tradition and our cultural heritage shape much of what we do, but we don't usually think of it in historical terms. Mostly we just keep on with "the way we do things around here." Our way is different from churches in California, New England, the Bible belt, and even the other side of town. What we, like all small churches, need to remember is that the way we do things is not the only right way, but simply our way.

Our stories and our traditions link the present congregation with our past. Each new pastor is told the story of the time that someone brought an alarm clock to church set to go off in the middle of a long sermon. It happened back in the 1930s, but it's still a reminder to the preacher to keep to the point. Remember the now-famous politician who dropped his marbles on the wooden floor as a child during a service? Our children are still like that, and he's proven that it won't keep them from succeeding in life. These stories belong to all of us, as we embellish them and pass them on.

Although a small church loves the contributions of the past, it should feel free to steal any good new idea that comes along. The palm crosses we fill with flowers at Easter were the idea of one interim pastor. The Christian Seder dinner was a tradition started by a pastor decades ago. The recent addition of a fall chicken barbecue seems to be a good home-coming celebration as we come back together after Labor Day. We've even been known to steal a good idea wherever we find it—visiting at another church, from a book or magazine, or from a conference speaker. Each "new" idea, once we see that it works for us, becomes part of our tradition and integrated into our identity.

Small churches may look completely change-resistant on the out-side, but, in fact, we're really of two minds about change. On one side, we don't want to throw away something that works as part of our ministry. After all, even after many years, we know how to do it and it still serves a constituency well. If a tradition has truly died, though, there's no point in trying to flog it back to life. For many years, we had a successful craft fair, showing work from many different craft folks. We no longer have people with the time, interest, and skill to work on the crafts, so we needed to let the fair go. To decide whether to keep or eliminate an activity, you need to ask the critical questions: "What is this contributing to the church's ministry?" and "Is the contribution worth the effort?" It takes courage to act on the answers, but it's worth it.

On the other hand, small-church people do like refreshment. We don't want to throw out our entire style of worship, but a change to some livelier music adds a welcome breath of freshness. Sometimes change is almost like the movie *Back to the Future*. You may find that so many things have been tried over the years that there's often a precedent for giving the next new idea a chance. Just because an idea didn't work in one generation doesn't mean it won't work today or tomorrow. Some of your new ideas, even though you've never seen them before, have the potential to strengthen the very things you're already doing.

WE DO SQUABBLE AMONG OURSELVES.

Yes, sin is alive and well even in the small church. Folks in a small church are different from each other, and sometimes those differences become the focus of attention. Sometimes, instead of resolving our problems openly, we just grumble. This is always a bad idea, because the emotional charge that builds up usually gets discharged on the wrong issue at the wrong time. Sometimes we will be able to resolve the core issue, and sometimes we just need to live with a situation that does not go our way.

Take, for example, the issue of children in worship. The theory is that including children in worship helps them grow into participating adults. In practice, children are often distractible, unable to sit still, and the cause of distraction to others in the service. The situation for parents includes both sides of the problem. On one hand, a mother would like her children to learn to be part of worship as they grow, and on the other hand she would like to be able to pay attention to the sermon and her prayers rather than having to keep an eye on her child.

It's important to address this kind of issue as soon as it arises. If you don't bring it out into the open, the community can fracture into factions without even noticing it. Grumbling leads to resentment, which can then lead to discovering other grounds to argue. As you help the parties involved work through to a solution, you need to create an atmosphere where each feels free to speak truthfully, to encourage the people with different points of view to hear each other, and to engage all the "sides" in problem solving.

In practice, we usually come up with a compromise that doesn't satisfy anyone completely, but addresses most everybody's concerns. Yes, the children can stay, but only for part of the service. Yes, we can provide a place where parents can hear what is going on without the child-sounds getting back to the congregation. But there will still be times when a preoccupied adult will wish a child would be quiet and also times when a parent will wish that his or her child could have been part of a special moment in worship.

Since we've lived together for many years, some of our conflicts have their roots in the distant past. Sometimes they are the result of the behavior of parents or even grandparents of the present congregation. Old arguments about a loan that might not have been paid back, a property line that was disputed, or work promised but not delivered are still real in the memories of the people. And because all sin and fall short of the glory of God, there are always new opportunities to argue about money, land, work, politics, friendship, courtship, and many other issues.

In a larger community, most of these kinds of issues arise with strangers, and it's possible to keep distance from our opponents. In the small-church community, many different kinds of interactions occur within the same circle of people, and as a result our opponent is also often our brother or sister in the church. This makes for complicated relationships, and people of a small church have many opportunities to demonstrate qualities of character like patience, empathy, integrity, and forgiveness.

WE LIVE IN AND THROUGH OUR RELATIONSHIPS.

In a small church, our relationships have ups and downs, but there is one deeply held conviction about life in the church: Even though we have our differences, what we hold in common is much more important than the things that divide us. Our relationships with each other, grounded in the love of God, are part of the air we breathe. Like a fish whose life is surrounded and maintained by water, we wouldn't be ourselves without the relationships within the church family that surround us and support us.

It's important to realize that this undercurrent of relationships is there if you're part of a small-church family. There are folks who care about you and how your day or your life is going, whether or not you have much in common. There are people who will support you and help you, even if they're not on your side in whatever issue you are struggling with. You are not alone, because the members of your church family are there for you. These kinds of relationships are completely the opposite of what is expected in our highly mobile modern culture.

To show you how this works in practice, let me tell you about the year we had only two girls in our congregation who were juniors in high school. They seemed very different on the outside, but both were deeply caring people of faith on the inside. Julie was pretty and popular with her peers—a cheerleader, a singer in the school musical, and an honor student. Anne was a gifted artist—already involved in fashion and jewelry design—a junior deacon in the church, and simply wonderful with small children.

The girls didn't have much in common or spend much time together outside of the church, but their lives were deeply entwined nevertheless. They were joined, not by shared interests, but by common values, personal caring and integrity, and shared experiences. Anne was devastated when we lost Julie to a traffic accident. "I've known her since I was born," she said. Julie's presence was part of the air we all breathed, whether we were admiring her talent or worrying about her short skirts. For all of the members of the church family, from the youngest to the oldest, losing someone who has been part of the family for an entire lifetime showed us how deeply our connection to each other is built into us.

We all feel for each other, day in and day out. When one part of our family hurts, we all hurt together. There are lots of ways to express that caring in a small church. When someone misses Sunday worship for a few weeks, folks ask each other if they're OK. When a family member is ill, a teenager is acting out, or a marriage relationship is under stress, feelings and reactions cross the congregation. We care, we pray, and, when we can, we try to do something to support each other. Cards, phone calls, casseroles, rides to the doctor, and doing errands are a few of the many ways we reach out when someone in the family is hurting.

Love is a feeling, but, more important, love is a willed intention to act for the good of the other person in the relationship. If you are living in a small-church family, chances are that you have lots of opportunities to express your love in caring acts. Watching, listening, and responding to other members of the church family provide lots of opportunities to practice and grow in ability to act out of love.

WE TAKE CARE OF EACH OTHER IN CRISIS.

When a small church is faced with a crisis, it reacts, not rationally with plans and reasons, but organically, as people reacting individually from the heart. Folks come forward spontaneously, offering whatever they are able to contribute. Each offers his or her own best, looking to find out what things need doing and then volunteering to do them.

We saw this in the way our whole community reacted to Julie's death in the traffic accident. I was away on vacation, a four-hour drive from the church, when Julie died. The accident happened at 4:30 in the afternoon, and I heard about it a little after six o'clock. At that time, one of our elders called from the church and said, "There's a bunch of people here. Should

I put on a pot of coffee?" "Of course," I said, "and put out some cookies, too." Another elder called two neighboring pastors, and they each came and stayed for a while with those who came to the church to grieve together.

When I got to the church after 11:00, there were still forty or so people in the church and on the lawn. More than a hundred folks had passed through—teenagers who were friends of Julie, friends of the family who wanted to offer support, and parents of other teens who felt the loss as if it were their own child. The word had passed around, through the instant messages and the cell phones, that folks were gathering at the church. This was where the community could find a safe place to meet, to react, and to support each other. No one needed to ask; everybody knew that this church is home for a family in crisis.

When it came time for the funeral, folks just stepped forward. "I think we're going to need more places to park. Should we use the field out back?" asked one man. He arranged for the grass in the field to be cut, got some traffic cones, and asked a friend to help him direct traffic. "We might not have enough room inside," so folding chairs were borrowed and speakers set up on the front porch. We were able to squeeze everyone inside for the service, but the outside space was a big help for those with little children who needed to run.

Even though school was out for the summer, the school psychologist came to teach us how to listen for teenagers in trouble. Leaders in the church came to listen and learn how to help those who might be most affected psychologically by the death of a peer. The music teacher from the high school, who brought fifty or so voices to sing at the funeral, took those teens to his own home afterward for mutual support. Gifts of hospitality and comfort, food and hugs and listening ears, were passed on from person to person, wherever a need appeared.

Each person who heard, whether a formal church member or not, came forward to do what she or he could. In a crisis, all petty issues were put aside, and caring action became everyone's priority. This kind of caring is not a carefully planned process; it is an instant reaction, straight from the hearts of the people. We are family, after all, and family takes care of family.

QUESTIONS FOR REFLECTION AND DISCUSSION

1. What is life like in your church?

2. How does your church resemble the lifestyle presented here? How does it differ?

3. How has God called you to be the church together?

4. What are the compromises you have had to make?

3

Worship Is at the Center of a Small Church

WORSHIP IS CENTRAL AND FORMATIVE.

ONE CONVICTION IS BONE-DEEP in our congregation: Scripture is what we stand on, what holds us together, and what forms us as a church family.

In a small church, worship is central and formative for the gathered community. For us, in our worship, the Scripture is the basis for everything we do. We listen to it, we pray about it, we sing about it, we struggle with how to apply it, and we commit ourselves to try to live by it. We respond to it by sharing the sacrament of communion together and by celebrating the major events of our lives together. Our worship brings us together as a church, and our worship is what defines us as a community—our values, our common goals, and the ways we try to live our lives together.

The first question of the Westminster Catechism, which is part of our Presbyterian confessions, asks what is the purpose of human beings. The answer is that our purpose is to glorify God and to enjoy God forever. It's in worship that we share the lived experience of belonging to God, of loving God, and of rejoicing in God. In worship, we orient ourselves together to God's presence with us. When we pray, either with words or with music, we are aware of coming into God's presence, turning ourselves toward God.

Any relationship requires continuing conversation to keep it alive, and our relationship with God is no exception. We talk to God in prayer, and we listen to God in Scripture. When we listen to the word in worship together, we're really listening for God's side of the conversation, to hear God's contribution in an active relationship.

If you're part of a small church, look carefully at the way you relate to the Scripture in worship. Is it something you've heard so regularly that you've stopped really paying attention, or is it today's part of a live conversation you're having with God? Your relationship with God is both individual, unique to the particular person you are, and public, as God enters into the circle of your church family.

Worship is a unique experience during the week of a small-church member. It's a time to put aside all the practical details that fill our minds the rest of the week. It's a time to lift our minds and hearts to look at the broader and longer-term implications of the lives we are leading. In one of my favorite quotations, the pastor of a small rural British church is described as "providing the inhabitants of Clare with their weekly ration of the abstract."[1] Worship is a time to set ourselves apart and to look at our lives through God's eyes, and perhaps to take action on what we see from there.

WORSHIP IS INFORMAL.

Worship time in a small church tends to be both informal and deeply emotional. If the "style" of a church could be compared to a restaurant, ours would be a comfortable, affordable, family-style restaurant, rather than an expensive, elegant, upscale "dining experience." We want to be ourselves in our worship, not pretend with sophisticated language or exaggerated manners that we're somehow better than we really are. For us, worship is expressed by bringing ourselves before God the way we really are.

This does not mean that we intend to show any disrespect for the Lord by the way we dress or the way we act. Quite the contrary. We bring before God our most sincere feelings—our love, our gratitude, our reverence, and our deepest humility. We're serious in our remorse and repentance over our sin. We're truly glad about the blessings we've received. We brush away a tear when a hymn like *In the Garden* touches our hearts. Sometimes we simply have to laugh at the irony of our human situation. Above all, we love the Creator who made us, the Son who rescued us, and the Spirit who stands by us.

There was a wonderful study, sponsored by the Alban Institute and the Lilly Foundation, of styles of worship in three different churches in

---

1. Tey, *Brat Farrar*, 200.

the same denomination. The researchers at Boston University visited and filmed worship at three Methodist churches—one suburban church, one inner-city African American church, and one small rural church. Watching the three worship experiences side by side gives a clear picture of what makes worship in the small church unique.[2]

The urban and suburban churches were both much more formal, with careful attention to details of music, dress, and formal roles in the service. The rural church was more informal in music, individualistic in dress, and almost spontaneously flexible in what different folks did. The rural church and the inner-city church both shared a deep emotional involvement in worship, particularly in prayer. The visible difference between them, in keeping with the less formal style, was that emotionality in the rural church was expressed in a restrained, almost understated, way.

The film of the rural church could easily have been made during one of our services. Our people typically dress informally, with more sweaters and shirtsleeves than suit jackets. Our music is more enthusiastic than precise. Children, or in our case teens, get to ring the bell after the service. We try to use hymns that folks know and love, and we take requests for favorite music whenever possible. Our children's message tends to involve feelings and what the Bible says about the way we should live. Our sermons use examples from the community's life and from the pastor's personal experiences. For us, too, the unexpected provides teaching moments that enrich the worship rather than interrupting it.

During the service for my installation in this church, for example, the unexpected happened during the hugging that always follows the laying on of hands and prayer. The communion table was set, and someone, probably me, knocked over the cup of grape juice. I took the moment to explain to the congregation what had happened, and that I had prayed that morning not to do anything stupid during the service. Just as I was offering that prayer, a mockingbird outside the window had let out with the most beautiful song. What I heard in the bird's song was that there was too much to be joyful about in this day to worry about silly mistakes. By the time I'd shared these thoughts with the congregation, an elder came in with a fresh cup, and the service went on. In a small church, you simply go with the flow and let the circumstance and the Holy Spirit lead.

2. Clark, *How We Seek God Together*, VHS video.

Our worship, like the rural church in the Lilly study, includes everyone. Parents, grandparents, and children are scattered across the congregation, sitting with their family members and friends. There is a certain sense of motion among the worshippers that you don't usually see in other styles of worship. Children move around, adults get distracted by their own thoughts, and seniors need to stretch stiff knees or visit the restroom. I believe that we're just a little bit more wiggly and physically free than our more formal counterparts, because, after all, we are among family.

SHARING CONCERNS IS COMMUNICATION IN THE FAMILY.

The time in the worship service that we call "joys and concerns" is when we share with our church family the events and concerns of our lives. Yes, we ask for prayer for our friends, relatives, and coworkers who are having medical problems or have had major losses in their lives. We offer thanks when the news comes back that the situation has been resolved. Sometimes we celebrate apparently miraculous healings or diagnostic "misunderstandings," and sometimes we pray for the families of those who have died. But "joys and concerns" goes far beyond this.

This is when we share our milestones and joys within the family. Here we introduce our visiting families, and here we embarrass each other with birthday congratulations. Here we announce the news from distant friends, and here we update the family on our folks in nursing homes. Everyone is free to jump into the sharing

One of our regular visitors, an older lady who was really a Catholic by conviction but came to worship anyway, had a very soft voice, almost never heard in a service. She was a gifted and published poet, but a very private person. It was an electric moment in the congregation when she rose to share that her grand-niece was graduating from high school and had received a major award. We rejoiced with her, and we were also quietly glad that she had felt comfortable sharing her joy with us.

Sometimes our younger folk have something they want to share, and this is always a big day. The sharing time happens after the sermon, and younger children usually go downstairs for an activity during the sermon. An announcement from one of the younger children means that he or she needs to listen to come back upstairs when it's time to share. Kevin was about five when he came back into the sanctuary for a very important an-nouncement. He had a brand new cousin! Actually, this was his third new cousin, but this one was a boy! He was thrilled, and we all were thrilled to share his enthusiasm.

Our sharing of concerns and our empathy for each other form a deep bond within the family. Life-changing events, good and bad and sometimes some of each, come to light here. This is where a new grand-child is announced, not as born or adopted, but as "found," the result of a relationship that did not include marriage, but a child to be loved and welcomed into the family nevertheless. This is where a devoted wife and mother can say, "My husband left me," and know that whatever kind of support she asks for will be forthcoming.

Critically important times of our lives first cross the airways here. This is where we can admit that our relationships are rocky, our loved teen has had trouble with the law, or the health issue we've been fighting for years is not getting any better. This is where a beloved mother within the church can say, "The tests came back, and it's cancer," and know that we will all be with her as she passes through it.

When we bring a concern, we can be sure that prayer for our issue is deep and sincere, as our prayers are for the concerns that we hear. We know that each member of our family will support us in need, just the way we know we will support those whose troubles we pray for. We may be close friends or not, and we may have things in common or be very different. Those superficial things don't matter. What matters is that we are family, and that our hearts are with any member of our family who is suffering, for whatever reason.

There is often an impatience with the amount of time spent sharing joys and concerns. Because it's not predictable, you may find that folks who like to stay on schedule become uncomfortable. Sometimes, it may feel like the issues are trivial or the people mentioned are somehow dis-tant. But the reality is that, if someone feels strongly enough to want to share, the issue is important to them and deserves respect. This may be the one place a person feels that others will care enough to listen and hear what's in their heart.

One very effective way to arrange this time of prayer is, rather than having the pastor respond to requests, to have the people pray for each other. Using an overhead projector, it is possible to list the requests as they are made, and, after each one, ask for a volunteer to offer that prayer.

Then, with the issues and the names of the volunteers on the screen, the volunteers can pray for each of the requests in turn.

The beauty of this approach is that folks learn very quickly that public prayer is something anyone can do, that there's no right way to pray, and that each person speaks to God as whoever they are. It is wonderful to hear adults pray for a child's issue and to hear children pray for a peer or a grown-up. When you pray for someone else, especially someone you've had a problem with, it touches your own heart in a way you would never expect.

WORSHIP IS PRACTICAL.

Preaching is critically important in a small church, because it provides the basic context for all of the other activities of our life together. As people of God through Jesus Christ, we need to listen to God's word in order to know what God has in mind for us. Preaching provides the link between the Scripture and our day-to-day reality by helping us figure out the meaning of the scriptural stories and commandments in our own environment and by giving us illustrations and implications to show us how to apply it.

We are striving to be followers of Jesus. As Dietrich Bonhoeffer points out in the introduction to *The Cost of Discipleship*, this means that we are engaged in "a more determined quest for him who is the sole object of it all, for Jesus Christ himself." According to Bonhoeffer, what we need to hear from a sermon is quite specific to our situation:

> What did Jesus mean to say to us? What is his will for us today? How can he help us to be good Christians in the modern world? In the last resort, what we want to know is not, what would this or that man, or this or that church, have of us, but what Jesus Christ himself wants of us. When we go to church and listen to the sermon, what we want to hear is his Word.[3]

Preaching is the link between the principles of Scripture and the reality of life around us, and that preaching connects these two worlds. As we listen to God's word in worship in a small church, we receive practical guidance that relates to how we use our time during the rest of the week.

Every preacher has his or her own way to think about the contents of a sermon. For me, a sermon includes four elements—engagement, con-

3. Bonhoeffer, *The Cost of Discipleship*, 35.

tent, context, and challenge. This is a checklist rather than a formula, since the elements can appear separately or mixed, in any order. Engagement usually comes first, to make it interesting and get attention—for instance, thinking about what it feels like to be part of the story, considering an incident when the passage was particularly relevant, or even exploring a conflict over the possible meaning of the message. Content refers to what the passage meant to the one who first said it and the ones who first heard it, context is what that message means in modern terms, and challenge refers to what we will do differently because we have heard it. You'll notice that three out of four elements include links to practical experience.

The practicality of worship includes understanding both the principles in the message and the ways we can apply them. It's critically important that the calls to action as a result of what we hear are possible—actions we can actually take within the constraints of our existing lives in the community. We know we'd all like to see peace on earth and an end to all war and violence. We do pray for peace and vote when we have the chance, but we aren't usually consulted on national policy. We need to find ways to be effective in response to what we hear.

In a small church, it's important to live by the old principle, "think globally, but act locally." We may not be able to advise the U.S. president, but we can have a significant impact on gang violence or racial tensions in our local high school. We can't help all the poor, but we can find few of those who are suffering for whom we can make a difference. We can't be advocates for all the social issues we care about, but we can focus our energies on a few selected causes where we can have an impact.

As the pastor engages the people in worship, he or she is providing the connection between the Scripture, the word of God, and daily life. This doesn't mean that one offers a to-do list of specific actions, but that all the listeners are helped to discern what God is calling them to do and be as individuals. I remember one man in the new members' class when I first joined the church, saying, "I don't want to be told what to do. I want to know what the Scripture says and then I can figure out for myself what I'm supposed to do about it." Doing this involves encouraging people to think theologically, but in a very practical way.

WORSHIP IS EMOTIONALLY ENGAGED AND PERSONAL.

We do love the God who created us and the Lord who saved us from ourselves. We feel joy, gratitude, unworthiness, relief, sorrow, empathy, compassion, and many other things during our time of worship. However comfortable or uncomfortable we are with showing our feelings, worship is an appropriate time to experience them and express them.

Sometimes we find tears in our eyes, and sometimes we are filled with awe. Sometimes we feel deeply unworthy of grace, and sometimes we feel like laughing because we are so incredibly blessed. We don't think of ourselves as demonstrative people, but often what we experience during worship touches us somewhere deep in our souls. Sometimes we're torn between the feelings that well up inside and our desire to respect Paul's instructions that "all things should be done decently and in order" (1 Cor 14:40).

In our music, we're able to express our feelings in a way that can be private and personal, but also shared with the rest of the church family. Each of us seems to have one or two traditional hymns that touch deeply, often based on special associations. For me, *The Church's One Foundation* brings grief over conflicts within the church. For another, *I Love to Tell the Story* expresses a lifelong theme of sharing the gift of faith. For several, *I Come to the Garden Alone* brings back the memory of God's presence with them in very dark times.

The classic hymns of the church resonate with deep feelings that are alive in us still. *O Come, O Come Emanuel* is a call for the presence of God. *Be Thou My Vision* is a plea for God's leadership that we raise over and over again. We sing *Silent Night* in reverent wonder at the coming of the Christ child, and we sing *Jesus Walked That Lonesome Valley* aching to reach out and soothe his pain at the end.

We also sing modern praise songs to express our feelings in worship. *Shine, Jesus, Shine* and *Shout to the Lord* are ways to celebrate the presence of Jesus in our lives. *Holy Ground* brings us to reverence as we are reminded of his presence, and *You Are My King (Amazing Love)* lets us feel the emotional impact of his sacrifice for each of us. We can even let the love in our hearts overflow as we sing *I Love You, Lord*. This kind of music allows us to worship with our feelings quite explicitly.

How do you let the people of your small church feel freer to express their feelings in worship? Find out the music they love. The best way I know is to have a hymn sing and encourage people to make requests.

It doesn't matter if you have a musician who's able to take spontaneous requests or if you need to ask for requests a week in advance. You will be amazed at the ways our hymns have deep meanings for different members of the congregation. Do keep records of people's favorites and weave them into worship as the feelings evoked are appropriate.

Do also let your people experience the effects of very different music styles. Dietrich Bonhoeffer brought African American spirituals from the black church he served in New York City back to his German seminarians in the 1930s, and his students always remembered the way that music engaged them more deeply in worship.

There are lots of varieties of music to choose from, and each has its own unique flavor and perspective. The African American spirituals like *I'm Gonna Live So God Can Use Me* express an active commitment, while the Taize chants like *Jesus, Remember Me* lead into meditation and a sense of God's presence. Each of the church's ethnicities has made its contribution. I particularly love the way the perspective in *The Church's One Foundation* was translated into Chinese and came back into English as *O Christ, the Great Foundation*. Exploring the choices to find the ones that appeal to your own congregation is a great adventure.

When we're engaged in our relationship with God, we all know that being deeply moved in worship is to be expected from time to time. Out of respect for each other, we need to learn when our neighbor needs a hug and a listener, or when to respect their personal space. Usually, though, we smile a bit, because we know that whatever our neighbor is experiencing, we, too, have experienced at one time or other. We thank God for the softening of heart that allows us to care for God and for each other so deeply and freely.

QUESTIONS FOR REFLECTION AND DISCUSSION

1. What is the most important part of worship for your church?

2. What makes worship most significant for you? What helps you move into the experience of worship?

3. What parts of your worship style do you agree on? Where do you differ from each other?

4. How familiar are folks in your church with the Bible? Who reads and uses it regularly?

5. How open are you to sharing feelings and life events in worship? What encourages or constrains your sharing?

4

In a Small Church, Everybody Does Ministry

LEAVING MINISTRY TO THE STAFF DOESN'T WORK.

WHEN A SMALL CHURCH looks at larger churches, people imagine that everything would be OK if the small church could only afford enough staff to do what needs to be done. Often, as happened at St. Andrews, we just hope that the right new pastor will make everything better:

> St. Andrew had a bad case of clericalism. It placed its hope for renewal on the pastor. "We need a charismatic leader to turn this thing around" was the rallying cry. But it discovered that small churches can turn things around only if the people take complete ownership of the church's administration and ministry.[1]

In a small church, the situation quickly becomes obvious: You simply can't afford to pay enough for professionals to do all the work that needs to be done. Often, the church can only afford the most minimal pastoral coverage: someone to lead worship and provide basic pastoral care. In other areas, whether it's cleaning and painting, correspondence and copying, planning and organizing, or teaching and leading, work that a small church can't afford to pay for still needs to be done.

Small churches depend on volunteers because there's nobody else to do the work. I knew that I was in an effective small church when our treasurer said, "The day when we have to pay someone to copy the bulletin is the day this church might as well close." This church runs on the work of its people, and that's simply the way it is. Whatever ministry gets done in

---

1. Bliese, "Life," 26.

a small church gets done because the people of the church do it. Pastors come and go, but the people make the work of the church happen.

If you see something that you think needs doing around the church, and it matters to you, you'll probably be the one who ends up doing it. If you're thinking clearly, you'll probably get a couple of friends and a new-comer to help. If you bring some coffee or iced tea and a snack, what you'll have is a party with a purpose. You'll find that work gets done, friends get to enjoy each other's company, and you get to know the person behind the new face. You can make whitewashing the fence into an event you might like to do again next year.

The economic reality of life in a small church is that real people need to do real work. This might sound like a problem, but actually it's a very good thing. When ministry can't be handed off to paid staff or even a regular worker group, then it's clear that everybody is needed and every contribution matters.

THE SMALL CHURCH WORKS ORGANICALLY AS A WHOLE.

A small church really is like the body, which Paul uses to illustrate the way different gifts are used in the church. When the church acts, it acts as a single entity, rather than as the different contributions of its individual parts. Decisions are made by the community as a whole, and everyone participates in the decision-making process, whether or not they come to agree with the final decision.

The ultimate authority in a small church actually belongs to the congregation as a whole, even though the pastor or deacons or elders may have nominal authority in particular areas of the church's life. This is because, in a small church, the people either do the work required to get things done, or they choose not to do it. People want to know about what's going on in every area of the church, whether or not they're directly in-volved. If you can find a way to include everyone's input and make the decision-making process visible, you're on the way to making a decision that can be accepted even by those who don't favor it.

One of the issues about which everyone has an opinion is the time of the worship service. We try to move the service to an earlier time during the summer because the church gets warm very quickly on a hot day. One year, there was suddenly a lot of resistance to the earlier time. Everyone seemed to be able to think of someone else who had trouble coming to church early. The elders supposedly have the authority to decide the service times, but I wanted to find out the basis for the resistance.

The rumor that I heard said that some of the older folks had trouble getting up early. I called Klaus and Bridget to see if it bothered them. "No," they said, "We're always up early. But Becky has to take care of her husband in the morning." When I called Becky, she said she was fine with the early time, but she thought that Jane might have a problem. When I talked to Jane, she said that if it was a good day, the time didn't matter, and if it was a bad day, being earlier or later didn't matter either. A full survey around the congregation showed that, while folks were concerned about each other, no one actually had a problem with the earlier time slot. In the end, though, everyone was relieved that I could say with certainty that a 9:30 service didn't pose a hardship for any of our families.

Regardless of who has ultimate authority for a decision, successful actions in a small church involve a consensus process that engages the whole congregation. This is because, in a small church, power and authority reside with the people rather than the pastor. The pastor acts as a teacher, and the pastor is able to influence the congregation through interpretation and application of the Scripture. The pastor is also an encourager, a supporter, and a guide for individuals in the congregation.

However, a pastor does not have the effective power to direct a congregation against its own convictions. This realization can be a shock to pastors who have a strong belief in their pastoral authority, but the reality is that the pastor has only the authority earned through teaching and personal example. The people will make their own decisions, either with the pastor's effective help or without it.

Because a small church lives through its relationships, even the work of ministry is relationally driven. This means that, in any particular activity or task, relationships matter more than performance or organization. In practice, this means that the poor, dying plant can't make its way to the dumpster until you're sure that that plant isn't important to someone. It means that, even if a person isn't particularly good at what they're doing, it's important to help them move to an alternative ministry where they can succeed, rather than "firing" them to make the way for new ideas.

The small church, when it's working well, is a whole that needs to respect and protect all of its parts. It makes decisions as a whole, acts as a whole, and allows space for each person to participate. It doesn't respond to arguments about efficiency, about better ways of doing things, or about effectiveness, unless the people involved and invested in the work of ministry are considered and cared for.

If you spend much of your life in business environments, this can feel incredibly frustrating. This kind of organic, relational process doesn't mean that change isn't possible. It does mean that changes grow out of relationships, evolving as individuals make adjustments in the pattern of their activities together.

EVERYBODY HAS ONE OR SEVERAL JOBS IN THE CHURCH.

Because the small church is always shorthanded, it's important to use all of the gifts and talents of all of the people. This means that there's a place for everyone to use their gifts among the many different kinds of work to be done.

The work of the church is inclusive in the broadest sense: There is something for everyone to do, regardless of real or perceived limitations. If it's hard to get out at night, there are things to do in daylight. If you have a job that makes you work most Sundays, there's ministry to do during the week. A person who is shut-in can still send birthday cards, and a mother with small children can still send get-well cards. One who works in a garden store arranges for Christmas and Easter flowers, and one whose office is near the wholesale distributor orders the palms for Palm Sunday. Those who cook well, of course, are the backbone of fellowship events.

Two women of our congregation, Betty and MaryAnn, both have the gift of being able to work with flowers. Betty once had a florist business, and for special events, especially luncheons and funeral receptions, she makes exquisite floral centerpieces that often appear on the tables. MaryAnn does wonderful things with silk and dried flowers. As the seasons change, wreaths or baskets matching the colors of the season appear on each of the double doors to the sanctuary. The baskets of purple flowers for Lent, suddenly and without notice, sprouted additional white lilies on Easter. Neither Betty nor MaryAnn talks about what she does; each one simply does it and does it beautifully.

Some of those who are able to drive have a ministry giving rides to those who cannot. Ralph moved to the area several years ago to be near his son's family. He moved into a senior housing apartment and found himself in high demand in the complex, taking his neighbors to the grocery store. He became a deacon in the church, visiting many friends and neighbors in the hospital and nursing homes. His warm smile and his kindness won him many friends in the community, even though now his driving ministry is behind him.

Special programs in the church tend to have advocates who make them happen. Lucy and Sally organize and sponsor two memorial blood drives each year. Becky organizes and runs the annual yard sale, an event of gargantuan proportions for our small community. Susie makes the banners to commemorate the communicants' classes. Sarah provides music for children. Dan takes wonderful pictures for the church newsletter. The church values (and needs) every contribution—those that are seen as well as those that happen quietly behind the scenes.

One Sunday, we declared an attempt to clean out the attic of the church, since an opportunity was offered to have things hauled away. I asked Don, who can tell antiques from spare lumber, and Greg, who can tell pageant props from trash, to direct traffic. I asked Jed, Mark, and Eddie, our strongest teenaged boys, to be available. At the beginning of the service, I asked those who could to stay after coffee hour to do some transporting. I was amazed at the crew who stepped forward. The men brought things to the steps, the teens brought them down, and everyone else, from grade schoolers to grandparents, moved them to the dumpster or the curb. Even folks who were completely new to the church pitched in, and there was a lot of laughing going on.

One year, I decided to give pins to everyone who had served the church as an officer or service provider of some kind, and almost everyone in worship that day had a reason to stand and come forward. Now, although we try to recognize everyone, I only have to give pins to those few who are the new contributors each year. It's nice to see a continuing flow of these new contributors and for the new people to see that they're becoming part of an active group which includes all of the rest of the community.

One of the folks who come to our Wednesday dinner program was rinsing something at the sink in the kitchen during the clean-up. She said, "You can tell that you're not company any more when you're allowed in the kitchen." A small church needs to make everyone feel comfortable enough to pitch in and enjoy sharing the work.

Sometimes in a small church, you get into the habit of asking the same people for help when something needs to be done. Including everyone in the work by finding some aspect of our shared work that each can do spreads the burden so volunteers don't get burned out. It also allows those who aren't often asked to share the satisfaction of making an important contribution.

ANY BIG PROJECT NEEDS EVERYBODY'S HELP.

For a small church to undertake a big project, whether it is a fundraising event, a mission project, or an educational program, the support and participation of everyone are needed. When a major effort is on the horizon, everybody knows they'll be called on, and folks plan their participation early. The two biggest events in our church year are the annual yard sale, traditionally the Saturday before Fathers' Day, and Vacation Bible School.

Our Vacation Bible School, or VBS as it's called for short, is a half-day program for children that happens for a week in the middle of July. Typically, we have about as many children as we have regular attendance in worship: somewhere between thirty-five and fifty-five children. It's offered for a nominal charge to the families of the community. Many children begin as preschoolers and then become assistant leaders when they reach junior high and high school age. Most of the participants are neighbors or visitors who aren't even affiliated with the church.

VBS is a major undertaking. There are typically four activity centers—Bible story, mission, crafts, and recreation—and the groups of children move from one to another during the morning. There is an assembly time with music at the beginning and end, a snack period each day, and an evening program on Thursday night for families. Adults lead each of the activity areas, and assistant leaders accompany the groups of children from place to place.

Can you imagine the kind of staffing a program of this size needs? There are leaders for assembly, music, snack, Bible, crafts, mission, and recreation; there's organization and training for assistants; and there are registration table folks to get children into the appropriate groups. There's a puppeteer for the mascot of the year and a person to ring the bells for activity changes. There are materials needed to support every activity—craft materials, game props, and Bible story scenery. There's even a team (whose jobs keep them from coming during the day) to make the sets that transform the sanctuary into a ranch or a forest or a lighthouse, depending on the theme of the materials for the year. And, of course, there's an overall director to pull the whole thing together. It is an exhaustive and sometimes exhausting enterprise.

One year, when the need for VBS volunteers was announced, the response was underwhelming. The director looked at the long list of tasks, and there was no way that the short list of people who had come forward could handle them all. She made one final announcement during the service that Sunday: "If I don't have enough people by noon today to do the VBS, we'll have to cancel it for this year."

This was exactly the right way to present the problem, and the congregation was exactly the right group to present it to. If the church as a whole no longer thinks that it's worth the trouble to present Vacation Bible School, then stopping it is the right decision. How does the decision get made? The decision is made by the people who choose to give their time, or not to give their time, to make the program happen. That year, the director had more than her full complement of volunteers well before the end of coffee hour.

Any big project—a yard sale, a community dinner, a street fair, or a Bible school program—needs one or two people to take responsibility for organizing and directing it. The leader isn't responsible for doing the work, but for organizing it. Organizing includes figuring out which activities need to be done, inviting people who might enjoy those activities to participate, making sure that each participant knows what his or her role entails, making sure that materials and helpers are available, and making sure all participants feel appreciated for their contributions. The leader is the cheerleader as well as the coach for the team, bringing the project together so everyone can have a good time and share in the success.

TRADITION, CULTURE, AND HISTORY
LEAD IN ALL OUR PLANNING.

Like the biblical people of Israel, the people of a small church live in a cyclical and seasonal tradition. Our seasons and the activities of our community are led by the events of the ever-circling year. We begin at Advent, preparing for the entry of God into the world at Christmas. This is a season of beginnings, and our first memories in faith often circle around the coming of the Christ child. After the long darkness of winter, we come to acknowledge our weakness and our sin during Lent, beginning with the ashes of Ash Wednesday. Each year, we follow Jesus on the journey to Jerusalem and to the cross, through the triumphal entry on Palm Sunday, through the poignant last supper with the disciples, through the torment and abandonment of Good Friday, to the joyous day of resurrection and celebration at Easter.

Our life of worship is defined by the two great festivals of Christmas and Easter, and by the other events that we share with Jesus and his disciples as each year progresses. The ebb and flow of our church activities is defined by the seasons, occasions, and lessons of the scriptural cycle.

To that cycle we add the other significant transitions of our year—the return to school and work after the refreshment of summer, a time to give thanks for our blessings at harvest, the time to receive with joy those who have chosen to join our congregation, a time to recognize the growth of our children and the work of our volunteers, and special days for mothers, fathers, and grandparents. To these we add occasions of special significance to our congregation, like Boy Scout Sunday and the days for traditional mission appeals. Is it any wonder that our life together is full of traditions?

When we begin to plan the coming year, it is much simpler to start with last year's calendar than to begin with a blank page. This doesn't mean that the items on last year's calendar will automatically happen in the same way they did last year, or even happen at all. Was the Thanksgiving Eve service poorly attended? Let's reconsider whether we should hold it at all. We haven't had a Seder dinner in years, and people have said they miss it. Let's put it back on the calendar. Do we really need to do the yard sale again? Yes, as long as Becky wants to do a yard sale, we will have a yard sale. And so it goes, with all the contributors advocating for events and activities they care about.

It is not that we never change. We do like to freshen up old traditions, try out new ones, and leave behind those that have outlived their constituencies. But we do always begin our planning with our existing traditions, because that way we don't risk losing some aspect of our lives together that's important to some part of our church family. As you plan for your year's events, you'll find that some are treasured traditions, some are a pain, and some are a little bit of both. You should never be afraid to ask, "Why are we doing this?" or, "Who cares about whether we do this or not?" Sometimes you'll find that an event has lost its constituency, but is kept on because it's "always" been done this way.

Adding one or two new events each year and sprucing up one or two of the old standbys is one way to keep participation fresh and activities interesting. Encouraging people to speak freely, both about positives and negatives, will give you clues about when to try a new approach or when to drop an activity that's no longer effective. Encouraging folks to read, to visit other churches while on vacation, and to listen to what other churches are doing can bring in a flow of new ideas to try. Do enjoy the process of experimenting from time to time, even when what you learn is *how much better you liked the old way.*

THERE ARE ALWAYS ISSUES WITH OWNERSHIP AND TERRITORIALITY.

Yes, in the volunteer world of the small church, there is always the potential for conflict over ownership and territory. When a person originates an activity or an event, of course, it bears the style and preferences of its originator. But in my experience, the danger of an event becoming "my" event which has to be done "my way" is less of a threat than you might expect in the small church.

The reason for this is that people in a small church are used to working together on each other's projects, and that, if you want helpers, you need to allow the helpers to make their distinctive contributions, too. Those who insist on doing something exactly their own way usually end up doing the work alone. This takes the fun and fellowship out of the work, and everyone knows how it feels to be left alone in the kitchen to clean up.

Sometimes, though, an activity really will outgrow the perspective of its originator/advocate, and this is an opportunity for a church leader or pastor to intervene gently. If the way that a ministry is done truly compromises its effectiveness, it's time for the leader or advocate to learn a new approach. Usually, if the old approach is not working, the leader is already aware that things are not going well.

For example, if adult Bible study material has always been *taught* rather than *discussed,* the leader may have noticed that fewer and fewer people are attending regularly. The leader probably wants to be more effective, but doesn't know where to begin. You can propose rotating teachers and using different presentation styles to take some of the pressure off of the present leader. Suggesting a "new way" that is better than the "old way" is guaranteed to evoke resistance, but starting from the notion of improving on what has worked in the past is more likely to be received as helpful.

No matter how folks defend their territory, you should always try to enable success rather than to create a perception of failure. The goal of participation in church activities is to live our discipleship most fully in the context of the church family. Sometimes, a leader has been involved in an activity for so long that it's no longer satisfying, but no one is available to take over. Sometimes a leader needs a change of focus—maybe a chance to go from being a Martha to being a Mary or vice versa. It's an honor to be able to disciple a newcomer into a role you already do well, in order to make it possible to take on a new challenge or exercise different gifts.

It's a critical part of the role of the pastor and lay leaders to equip the people of a small church for ministry. This includes helping them to discover when their attachment to a particular aspect of ministry is getting in the way of their continuing growth in Christ.

QUESTIONS FOR REFLECTION AND DISCUSSION

1. What proportion of your folks is active in the church? Is there a core group that does most of the work?

2. How do you decide when to take on a big project?

3. When changes in the things you plan to do are proposed, do you find it interesting or threatening?

4. How do you end activities that are no longer productive?

5. How do you find opportunities in the church that match personal constraints and life situations?

PART II

Work and Activities of the Small Church

5

What Small Churches Do Uniquely Well

IF YOU ARE PART of a small church, you probably have looked envi-
ously at the beautiful music, the polished education offerings, and the
numbers of children to be found in larger churches. Don't worry. There
are things that small churches can do, ways of living out our commitment
to Christ, which our small, relational environment encourages. We are
blessed in ways that our larger neighbors may not even recognize.

SMALL CHURCHES ARE BANDS OF DISCIPLES.

To begin with, a small church is a place where people have unique opportunities to grow in their Christian faith and practice. New Christians
interact with experienced Christians, and experienced Christians learn by
living with others who have an extraordinary depth of faith. Discipleship
is like apprenticeship, happening in the context of an ongoing, day-to-day
relationship between role model and student.

Every person is involved in making disciples in two ways: Each one
receives guidance and help from those who have gone before, and each
one can offer help and support to those who are coming along. As we learn
and grow, we model what we have learned and pass it on to others. The
beauty of it is that, in a small church, you are participating in both sides
of the process of making disciples—you are learning from those around
you, and you are passing on what you have learned by demonstrating it
and explaining it.

Because of our close relationships in a small church, we know where
to go in the church for specific needs. You know where to find the prayer
warrior whose quiet confidence leads you through your response to doubt.
You know which of the business professionals have struggled with ethical
issues in their work. You have watched the quiet person who let the Holy

Spirit lead them into activities they never would have thought possible. You have listened to the gruff older gentleman who is full of common-sense wisdom about the human condition. You know, because you have seen them in action, that you have strong resources to go to when you are struggling with an issue of how to live out your faith.

In our education program, we come together to learn from Scripture, from experts, and from each other how to apply what we are learning in the situations we are facing. Our classes are small, and you can bring your own issues and concerns into the conversation. How should I handle it at work when my boss asks me to do something unethical? What should I do for an adult child who still seems to want to be taken care of? What do the basics of our faith really mean, anyway? How can I be a faithful Christian and understand the faiths of my non-Christian friends? Our concerns and situations are not new on the face of the earth, and we can help each other figure out how to approach them.

It is an honor when a wiser (and not necessarily older) person takes the time to listen, to dig into the depth of their understanding, and to offer you guidance from a fresh perspective. It is an even greater honor to have a person come to you to ask for the benefit of your experience and perspective in their own current struggle. Sometimes, the person who asks your advice may even be someone you have gone to in the past. Discipleship is a mutual activity, with us each offering help in the areas of our strength and each of us seeking out help in the areas where we most need to grow.

A small church, because of its longstanding relationships and the trust built up over the years among its people, is a place uniquely pre-pared for this kind of personal encouragement of discipleship. You can find that growing as a disciple while encouraging others in their faith is quietly happening on ordinary days in a small church. God is working in you, and you are doing God's work with your neighbors, without fanfare and without fuss.

WE CAN LIVE A COUNTERCULTURAL LIFESTYLE.

Another great advantage that small churches enjoy is their freedom. Churches can grow rapidly in two situations: when the needs that the church addresses in its community are growing, and when the community itself is growing. In both cases, the increase in the ministry of the church is a result of a growing trend in the surrounding culture. When the church is able to respond to that growth trend, the church grows. The "good old days" that many churches remember are usually one of those times when the church resonated with the situation of the popular culture and the surrounding community it served. Growth happens when the church is coupled with the interests and concerns of those around it.

A small church whose focus is on ministry rather than growth has an unexpected freedom. It can respond to the call of the gospel, rather than responding to or being directed by the needs and demands of the popular culture. As Richard H. Bliese pointed out in his article for Christian Century, our approach to ministry needs to use the advantages that small churches bring:

> Bigger congregations are almost always adept at tapping into significant cultural norms, values, movements and technology. This is their strength, but it is also their weakness. . . . The small church tends to be shaped more by the dynamics of its own small Christian community than by the dominant culture. . . . It can go places and risk ministries that larger churches would find undesirable or impossible.[1]

A small church, by recognizing that its success or failure is not measured by the number of people it pleases, is free to go about the work of Jesus Christ. And this work, by reflecting the eternal values of Christ, is paradoxically more likely to be effective in the bizarre world of the popular culture. In our area, for example, the places for singles to go were extremely limited. Like the singles environment described by Frank Tillapaugh,[2] ours was a bar scene filled with "good times" and casual sexual encounters. The church was able to provide, through its singles' group and informal dinners, a place to socialize that respected the personality, character, and values of the participants.

A small church, because it is free of the need to be led by the popular culture, is in a position to freely offer ministry that provides alternatives to that culture.

1. Bliese, "Life," 25–26.
2. Tillapaugh, *Unleashing the Church*, 83.

UNIQUE MINISTRIES COME THROUGH CONNECTIONS AND CONVICTIONS.

Small churches are also free to follow unique ministries that arise out of the personal connections and convictions of their people. Because small churches are more aware that they are not able to solve all the problems of the world, they can be less embarrassed to take on only a small part of those problems. When you realize that you can not solve huge problems with your limited resources, you are free to use the resources you have for the problems you encounter. One church with a member who came from Africa raised money for high school scholarships for students from her village. A couple who were moved by the children they saw on the streets in the Philippines began a decades-long program to support daycare centers there. You can be free of overwhelming expectations to respond to the specific needs that God brings to your attention.

For example, one small church has a conviction that its efforts should focus on local neighbors, so the results of special offerings usually go to the local food pantry and soup kitchen. Baskets in the entrance to the church collect food that also goes to the food pantry. The teens collected winter clothing for the homeless in the city, and the knitters make warm winter hats and mittens as well. As individuals, the members volunteer in programs in the area as their abilities make possible: driving for Meals on Wheels, greeting visitors at the hospital, and visiting shut-ins. The church becomes both an agent to help with local needs and a place to identify and share opportunities for individual service. You can provide the environment and mutual support for individual service very personally within a small church.

Ministries arise in the small church when the Holy Spirit leads a person to recognize and address a particular need. One church's evangelism began with enthusiasm for the Alpha program, an examination of basic Christianity that includes a dinner every week for ten weeks. Folks who came for the program enjoyed it so much that they wanted to continue, so they started an adult Bible study the same evening. Some singles who were coming to the Bible study decided that they wanted to have a study focusing on life as a single adult, so they became a separate study group. The program met for two sessions each year, in the fall and winter, serving dinner for twenty to thirty people every Wednesday night.

There are always more opportunities than a small church can handle arising out of our common life. You never know which corner the ministries will come from. Should we start some kind of support program for caregivers, since several of our people have been caring for loved ones with serious illnesses? Since two of the nurses in the congregation have just become involved with support for families of the mentally ill, should we do something with that? As each opportunity comes up, you think about it and pray about it, consider how you might rearrange the resources to cover it, and encourage those who arise as the advocates for that opportunity. Specific ministries always grow out of a specific need and a specific call felt by a particular member of the church family.

EACH PARTICIPANT REPRESENTS THE CHURCH.

If you are part of a small church, your identity becomes mixed up with the identity of the church. In a small church, each member and regular participant is identified with the church and the church is identified with them. You are always representing your faith, because you are always seen to be representatives of your church in the community. Who you are, what you do, and how you live are all seen as reflections of the church as a whole.

This close identification between the church and its people cuts both ways. If you behave badly, the entire church looks bad. If you are snobbish or judgmental, that image of the church quickly circulates around the community. If you are shy and withdrawn, the church will be known as a cold and unfriendly in-group. If you are involved in shady business dealings or petty conflicts, the whole church will be known as people who profess one thing and act another way.

The reverse is also true. If you are warm to strangers and include them in your conversations over coffee, the church's reputation will reflect your openness. If you give help and encouragement freely, the church you represent will be known as an encouraging place. Everything you do, from the way you respond to strangers to the way you cope with trials and losses, demonstrates to those who see you the difference it makes to be disciples of Jesus.

As you are known in the community, particularly as the church becomes known as people to come to in a crisis or for support and guidance, it is critically important that you are able to explain why you do what you do. As the apostle Peter says,

> Always be ready to make your defense to anyone who demands from you an accounting for the hope that is in you; yet do it with gentleness and reverence. (1 Pet 3:15–16)

When a person who is in need, in trouble, or in doubt comes to the church, you are the front line of the representatives of the kingdom of God on earth. You have the unique opportunity to bring God's love to someone who needs to know about it.

QUESTIONS FOR REFLECTION AND DISCUSSION

1. Given that all churches are unique, what does your church do particularly well?
2. Who helped you to grow in your Christian life? Whom have you encouraged over the years?
3. How does your church reflect the culture around you? How is it different?
4. Which church ministries have grown out of personal concerns and connections?
5. How does your community see your church?

6

Finding the Congregation's Priorities

WHAT DO WE DO NEXT?

Jesus came and said to them, ". . . make disciples of all nations, baptizing them in the name of the Father and of the Son and of the Holy Spirit, and teaching them to obey everything that I have commanded you." (Matt 28:18–20)

IT IS A LONG way from the great commission, or even from the carefully constructed mission statement of the local church, to knowing exactly what the people of the church will be doing in church this weekend or next Tuesday afternoon. How do you go from all the lofty ambitions for the kingdom of God to the actual to-do list for the next few days?

Even while the church's calendar of events is unfolding, specific work needs to be done in the church family every day of the year. Every day, we hope that each of our people is growing in faith and growing to be a little more like Christ. Every day, we want to make some little steps toward spreading the good news of God's love to those who haven't realized it. Every day, we want those we touch to come a little closer to Christ as his disciples. Every day, we want to do some of Christ's work in the world, reaching out to the poor, the oppressed, and the suffering. The prospect of trying to do all of these things on any given day can be overwhelming.

How do you discern your own particular local calling as part of the universal church? Of course, the process calls for prayer, because our goal is to discover God's will for us and not just make up something for ourselves. In the context of prayer and with the guidance of the Holy Spirit, it is up to each of us to use all of the resources of mind and heart to figure out what, specifically, God has in mind for us to do.

WHAT ARE THE POSSIBILITIES?

How do you even begin to think about what the possibilities for ministry of a small church might be? Often, because so much of what a small church does is a result of its history and its traditions, it can be hard to think of the range of possibilities that God might have in mind for its ministry. Jesus said to his disciples,

> For God all things are possible. (Mark 10:27)

We need to realize that, as few as we are and as familiar as we are with our limitations, what God may want to do through us may be beyond our wildest dreams.

One story, which comes out of the secular world, reminds me of the power that a small number of people can have in reviving an entire community. The novel *A Town Like Alice* by Nevil Shute is set in a dusty town in the Australian Outback, where the people dream of living in a "bonza" (excellent) town like Alice Springs. One young woman, by slowly introducing one activity after another over a period of years, leads their transformation into that kind of town—a town where people want to come and where natives are proud to stay. A small church, because of its long time horizon, deep understanding of the community, and perspective of the possibilities of God's kingdom, is in a very good position to lead this kind of transformation in its own place. By a consistent commitment to change, one slow step at a time, you have the ability to move your community toward the kingdom of God.

You may feel that the best your small church can do is to make lemonade out of the big lemon bearing down on it. In the 1960s, an old Scottish ghetto in Boston was faced with a migration that transformed their neighborhood into a largely black inner-city culture, complete with crime, drugs, and prostitution. The Presbyterian church there quickly welcomed the new families in the neighborhood into the church and into its leadership, resulting in a very strong African American church that reaches out for Christ to serve the needs of its evolving community.

The key for you, as part of a small church, is to look realistically at what is going on around you and then to look through God's eyes at the possibilities. This does not mean that you need to act like marketers and design a new product that will appeal to the largest segment of the market. It does mean that we look at the kinds of ways that the kingdom of God could break into our neighbors' lives, and then find a way that matches our abilities and our resources to help God make it happen.

HOW DO WE DISCOVER OUR GIFTS AND TALENTS?

I believe that God puts many of the clues to our calling in front of us: in the way we are made, in the inclinations and passions that God has placed in our hearts, and in the circumstances of the people of the world who are our neighbors. Your personal calling is most likely to be found at the place where your ability to serve and your God-given joy in the work match the needs of those in the world around you.

Paul places great importance on the fact that we each have different gifts and callings to different activities. He says,

> Now there are varieties of gifts, but the same Spirit; and there are varieties of services, but the same Lord; and there are varieties of activities, but it is the same God who activates all of them in everyone. To each is given the manifestation of the Spirit for the common good. (1 Cor 12:4–7)

The key things to note here are (1) that we are called to different services and activities based on our different abilities, and (2) that use of our abilities is not intended only for ourselves, but also for the common good.

There are a number of ways for you to approach learning about your spiritual gifts as members of a small church. There are secular aptitude tests, self-help books, and counselors to help you find out how your abilities might match the needs of paying jobs. There are Bible study guides and quizzes to help you identify the ways you might already be using the spiritual gifts that Paul talks about. There is also the witness of the community of faith, the people around you who let you know truthfully when you have done a gifted job and what other potential abilities they can see in you waiting to be tried.

Gifts and talents are not a static thing, decided once and for all. As you use them, your talents develop into skills, and you become better at what you do. As you use them, you may find some gifts deeply satisfying, while others, which you are equally good at, become boring or frustrating with long practice. Often, new gifts will emerge at different stages of life. For example, I know some folks who were not particularly good at working with children until they became parents or grandparents; those new encounters brought out sensitivities that had been sleeping all their lives. We need to assess our gifts continually to keep our knowledge of them current.

DEVELOPING OUR GIFTS TAKES PRACTICE.

One of the great advantages of the small church is its flexibility: There is plenty of room for people to try something new. We can try and succeed a little, and still the result is better than not having tried at all. In the small church, we do not measure results against perfection, but against what would have happened if we had not tried. To do a fair job on the first try is worth a celebration. To do a better job the next time is great. To develop a skill and then be able to teach it to others is fabulous.

Because there is so much to do in a small church, there are lots of opportunities to try out your different gifts. It is also possible to try out things you are not particularly good at, in the hope of getting better. For example, I am known to be domestically challenged and pretty hopeless in the kitchen. During one of our church's sessions of Wednesday night dinners, I volunteered for kitchen duty. To my amazement, I discovered I was able to reach a basic level of competence in organizing, cleaning up, and dealing with leftovers, which I had never expected. At every stage of life, you still have the opportunity to learn new skills.

The small church values generalists, people who are able to do a variety of things fairly well. The current trend in our culture, on the other hand, is to value specialization, the ability to do only a few things extremely well. I remember when I was a teen having a bicycle to get around. It was not a racing bike or a dirt bike, it didn't have fancy gears or tires, and I didn't have any special clothes with product logos to wear to ride it. My bike simply did what needed to be done, just like the volunteers and workers in a small church.

Learning to use your gifts in the small church, then, is just a matter of finding opportunities, volunteering, and getting out there. It is good to have someone to introduce you to the territory and be available for help with the unexpected, but small-church people like to be asked to help, especially when they don't have to do the whole job themselves. Learning and teaching go around and around in the activities of the small church as part of our ongoing discipleship process. Your gifts are needed, and you know how much you welcome others who are willing to share their own gifts.

WE NEED TO MATCH OUR GIFTS AND PASSIONS WITH THE NEEDS OF THE WORLD.

When Jesus raises the commandment to love our neighbor as ourselves to second greatest, coming only after our love for God, his listeners challenge him. Who, exactly, are we to love like that? The answer comes out of the story of the good Samaritan, but the answer to the question only appears at the very end of the story. Of all those who passed by the man in distress, who was his neighbor? The answer is, "the one who showed him mercy."

The needs of the whole world can be overwhelming for the people of a small church, who feel that they have barely enough resources to survive, much less to give away. Before the advent of the modern media, a church might only be aware of needs in its immediate area or of needs in foreign lands brought to their attention in stories from missionary travelers. It was possible for a young woman to become a teaching missionary in China in the 1890s, as my great-great-aunt did, when she heard about the need for teachers there. She was not aware of all the other villages in all the other countries that might have needed her services.

The number of appeals for money and participation that come even to a small church is staggering, and they are almost all worthy causes. How do you decide which needs call this particular church? How do you decide which of your worldwide neighbors you are able to help effectively?

I believe that a neighbor is someone with whom we have a connection, someone whom we can touch and someone who touches us in return. Because of our range of communications and ability to travel, that person might live almost anywhere in the world. As I said before while talking about the unique advantages of small churches, the best of our ministries grow out of our unique personal connections and convictions.

The people of each church have their own combination of connections and convictions. One church member I know has lived with multiple sclerosis for years and works as an advocate for the disabled. Another became an advocate for the mentally ill after she lived through her son's struggles with mental illness. Yet another became involved with a Native American group in the southwest, and she made her church aware of the needs in that community. Different churches in our area have connections with the struggles of illegal immigrants, the plight of migrant farm workers, the struggle to break out of addictions, the needs of unexpectedly pregnant mothers, and support for families of those in prison.

No one church can address all these needs, but we each can work with some of our neighbors when and where we encounter them. As you look around your own small church, you will find the seeds of many ministries in the existing connections of your own people. Who do you see struggling? Whose suffering touches your heart? Who needs the kind of help you can provide, whether it is the simple necessities of life, information and guidance through a process of healing, or advocacy for social justice? You will find the key to your most effective ministry is already living in the hearts and minds of the people of the church.

QUESTIONS FOR REFLECTION AND DISCUSSION

1. What are the current priorities in your church?
2. How do you consider the different kinds of possible activities and ministries?
3. How have you engaged God in prayer over your priorities? What has God indicated that you should continue to do or change?
4. Do you have a way of discovering gifts and talents? of developing your skills in practice?
5. How do you find activities that match and stretch each person's abilities?

7

Welcoming and Integrating Newcomers

FIRST, THEY NEED TO COME THROUGH THE DOOR.

Newcomers don't walk through the doors of our small churches very often. The last church I served was in a residential neighborhood, one which very rarely has new people moving in. We were not near a college or a major business center, or anything that would draw a steady flow of new people.

It's not that the people did not know we were there. The church is the biggest building in the neighborhood, right where the main road makes a turn at the top of the hill. People use the building as a landmark when they give directions. "You know, that big white church with the pillars, the one that has the big yard sale." Some people, like the Catholic woman who called to arrange for the funeral of her Protestant stepfather, feel that they're affiliated with the church just because they come to the yard sale loyally each year.

Even though the sign says Presbyterian, for most of the Catholics, Pentecostals, and lapsed just-about-everything-else who make up the neighborhood, we are just "some kind of Protestant." When someone new passes through our doors, they may as well have come from a foreign country, because the likelihood is that they have no idea what to expect inside.

New people do come through the doors every once in a while, and they come for a strange variety of reasons. They rarely come because of anything intentional the church has done, like the advertising in the newspaper, the fliers posted in shops, the invitations mailed out, or the neighborhood door-to-door canvasses. The only things that seem to work in inviting new people are prayer and personal invitations, and usually it takes both.

A sampling of the people who do come in the door on Sunday morning showed that they come for a variety of uniquely personal reasons. One man said he came because he has lived near this church for twenty-five years, and he wanted to see what it was like inside. He didn't come back. Others have come for only one visit because they thought this was the Pentecostal church down the hill. One longtime leader first came because her son was attending the nursery school program that used to meet in the basement. One person came when she learned her husband was having an affair, and another when his wife walked out on him. Another came because she was driving around looking for an Easter sunrise service, and this was the first one that she saw. One multigenerational family came first just to look and decided to stay because it "feels friendly" here.

This church tries to encourage building visitors, like the Boy Scouts, Girl Scouts, and Alcoholics Anonymous, to be comfortable in the space, especially in the sanctuary. Boy Scout Sunday turns out to be one of the most popular services of the year. Because of the range of participant faiths in the troop, the church does try to make the service open not only to the many kinds of Christians, but also to the Jewish leaders and their families.

There are many ways you can communicate a welcome when someone visits for the first time. You want to be friendly without putting the visitor into the center of too much attention. Asking the visitors if they would like to come in for coffee with you is much friendlier than inviting them to go for coffee into a room full of strangers. Some churches take new visitors a fresh-baked loaf of bread, with only a quick word to thank them for coming and to invite them to come back again. The message that seems to be received best by visitors to our small churches is that we enjoy your being here, but we don't want to be too pushy.

NEWCOMERS START AS FOREIGNERS, BUT THEY NEED TO BECOME FAMILY.

Because small-church people all know each other well, a visitor stands out in a worship service. The danger is for us to be too overwhelming, since everyone wants to shake the visitors' hands during passing of the peace, and everyone wants the chance to talk with them during coffee hour. Folks do seem to experience the church as welcoming and friendly, at least at first.

But how does inclusion in the church family actually happen? The common wisdom says that, because the small church functions as a family, a newcomer needs to be grafted into the family tree. Because this grafting takes time, it can be difficult for newcomers to move into inclusion in the family. It takes time to move from step to step, with the church getting to know the newcomers and the newcomers getting to know the different participants they see.

Moving from visitor to regular attendee is the second step in becoming part of the family, and it is up to the newcomer to make the decision to come back each Sunday. A perception of friendliness seems to be part of that decision, but the kind of experience the visitor has in worship actually seems to be more important. Comments range from "I can feel the presence of God here" to "this place is definitely not dead." Worship is the one thing that churches do that a seeker won't find in a social gathering, and the church's intrinsic connection with God is either perceptible to visitors or not.

Worship is the place where newcomers hear the gospel, and they see the gospel in action by becoming active with the members of the church family. For many of us, true conversion begins in that quiet moment when you suddenly realize that all you have been hearing really is true, and that it is true for you. Angels celebrate in heaven at that moment, but for many of us it is a quiet moment of sudden joy. I listened to sermons for six months in my own return to faith before I quietly accepted Jesus as my Savior as I sat in the pew one Sunday morning. Happily, you already have friends in the church family to share that moment with—friends who will understand because they have been there themselves.

Many people grow as Christians and attend a small church regularly for years or even decades without becoming more than a regular attendee. As a regular, one tends to have many acquaintances and a few friends in the congregation. Regulars participate in many church events, and some stick around long enough to be part of the church's legends and traditions. Some are simply commitment-phobic, and others still have a personal identity with the Lutheran, Methodist, Episcopal, or other church where they grew up.

Usually, regulars get involved in one or another activity for the church even before they actually consider becoming members. One new couple I remember edited and published the church newsletter, the husband taking candid pictures of church events, well before they joined a new member class. Another regular had been working with children in the Sunday School for more than two decades before she decided she was ready for membership. One man who grew up in the church played Santa for many years before he finally took the plunge into membership. Because there is so much to do in a small church, there are many ways to move from regular attendee to worker well before making a membership commitment to the church.

One church I served held new member classes in the fall, and any two requests to join would cause a class to be held in a particular year. All potential members, even those transferring from other churches, are encouraged to go through the class. Having a formal class or orientation for all gives those who are coming in a chance to understand who the church family is, personally and theologically, and where it fits into its denomination and its community. For example, a potential member should know where the church stands on the particularly divisive issues currently facing the churches in order to make an informed decision about what it means to become part of the family. Not everyone who takes part in a class should necessarily join the church, and no pressure should ever be applied to "encourage" new members who are not really ready for commitment.

WE NEED PLACES FOR NEW PEOPLE TO START.

Small churches need to have places for people to start—places where they can begin their journey into involvement in the church. There is always plenty to be done in a small church, but opportunities for new people need to be considered carefully. Work for new people ought to have some basic characteristics:

- It must be bounded—not an open-ended commitment that would make a person feel permanently tied to one place or role.
- It must be possible—something that an ordinary person can do and do well with a minimum of instruction and explanation.
- It must be visible—enough to give the person a sense of accomplishment and contribution.
- It must not need to be done perfectly—the person must be able to see that their best is good enough, and that there will be no comparisons with the way someone else used to do it.

- Church leaders must be able to let it go—no micromanagement is allowed when a person takes on a responsibility.
- Church leaders must be willing to accept anyone who volunteers.

The good news is that there are lots of activities that can fit these requirements. There are event-related activities, such as setting up the crafts for the Harvest Festival, running the games at the picnic, serving dinner for an evening program, setting up tables, or preparing the flowers for a dinner. There are child-related activities, such as painting sets for VBS, leading games, or making snacks. There are education-related activities, such as participating in adult Bible study, helping in a discussion group, or doing a presentation for the children's message in worship.

There are lots of activities you might not be doing just now, but which you would do if someone said, "Would you like me to take care of . . . ?" A talented gardener would make the grounds look much nicer. A flower coordinator would make the service flowers more consistent. A volunteer to plan activities for the younger children during worship would make childcare less hectic. There are many such tasks that thrive with willing volunteers, but can wait without much cost until someone else steps forward. Having an informal wish list of possible activities gives you some choices to offer newcomers who seem like they might enjoy being involved.

In addition, there are ways to encourage active contributions in an ongoing way. It helps when sign-up sheets for community pot luck meals include the kinds of things needed, whether a whole meal covered dishes, lots of hors d'oeuvres and finger foods, salads and desserts to go with a giant sandwich, or sandwiches to go with the soups for a Lenten meal. Everyone can be encouraged to contribute to coffee hour snacks, and for more formal meals, desserts are often requested and forthcoming.

The church kitchen is a place where people gather, and usually the person responsible for an event receives several offers of "What can I do?" from willing participants. Each chance to share the work is a chance to share the ownership of the church's hospitality. You can also encourage a sense that clean-up belongs to everyone, and that joining the team is part of the conclusion of an event. Since the fellowship hall has lots of uses, putting away tables and chairs after an event is usually needed, and folks can kindly get into the habit of cleaning up the space at the end of an evening. Newcomers can fit right in, working and joking along with the other members of the family.

THERE IS DANGER IN "DOING FOR,"
NOT INVITING TO "DO TOGETHER."

The biggest danger we face in integrating and assimilating new people is missing their willingness to be included in the work. There is a normal human tendency, when one is clearing the tables, to say, "It's OK, I've got it," when someone offers to help. We really mean well when we say, "Just sit and finish your coffee," but the message received is not what we intend.

If new people offer to help two or three times and are turned down each time, the clear message is that they are not needed. They may feel like honored guests, but they also feel excluded from the family. They may come to feel as if they were visiting in a home where all the action is in the kitchen, while they are only allowed to sit in the living room. In a small church, it's easy to tell that the laughter and conversation is going on wherever the volunteer crew is working. It's natural to want to be part of the action.

You really don't mean to have the newcomers feel left out, and you usually do the work yourselves out of the best intentions. But some of the greatest failures in inclusion result from this misunderstanding. To be truly welcoming is to accept the newcomer as a family member, like a kind of distant cousin whom we don't know well yet, rather than as a guest. In the family, we have a lot of fun when we get our hands dirty together. We need to remind ourselves that folks would rather participate in a good time than just sit and watch it.

QUESTIONS FOR REFLECTION AND DISCUSSION

1. How does your church invite newcomers? What works for you? What have you tried that didn't work?

2. How do you react to a new face? How does your reaction feel to the visitors?

3. What do you do to turn visitors into friends?

4. Where do people gather to "hang out" in your church? How can new people fit in?

5. What ways can new people contribute in order to "try out" being part of the church?

8

Conflict Is a Growth Opportunity

H AVE YOU EVER EXPERIENCED a conflict within your church? Do you think that you are alone in that experience? Have you fallen into the trap of thinking that, because the people of the church are God's people, they should have become immune to conflicts among themselves? The reality is that, even within the church, people still disagree.

CONFLICT DOES NOT FEEL GOOD.

One friend of mine is the pastor of a small church nearby. He is presently embroiled in a conflict within his church that has split the church into factions, one of which is represented by a very aggressive person with a strong agenda. When I heard about the mess, I gave him my usual sound bite about conflict: "Conflict in the church is God's training program to teach us to love people we don't like very much at the moment."

His response was insightful. He said, "You know, I've heard you say that before, but somehow it feels different when you're deep in the middle of it." He is exactly right. The real sense of conflict as a way to teach us to love the enemy in our face is very different from some theoretical statement about loving our enemies who are either stereotypes or far away. Loving your enemy in a small church is a very personal, gut-level activity.

You can choose your friends, but you can't choose your relatives. As Christians, we are all relatives, children of God and brothers and sisters of Jesus. In a small church, we are all close family, and so we need to live with each other, whether we happen to feel like it or not. Even more important, we need to love each other and support each other regardless of our current issues with each other.

When I came to my first church, the congregation was deeply split, almost in half, over the issue of how to hold services during the summer. One group wanted to share services with other churches in town, taking turns to host specific Sundays. The other group wanted to worship at home, and ended up hosting worship in the back yard of one of the members. When I arrived in September, neither group was sure whether they were ever going to be able to live together again.

My first sermon had a good news/bad news component. The good news was that the summer (and that particular fight) was over. The bad news was that there always will be something to fight about. The church was blessed that folks who were on opposite sides of the conflict were able to come together and work together again, although each person is still the unique and crotchety person he or she always was.

The first steps in coming back together were prickly and uncertain, but former opponents worked very hard to treat each other with respect and to give each other the benefit of the doubt. People's opinions and positions did not change, but their way of responding to each other did. I loved hearing a person from one side of the conflict say of someone who had been on the other side, "He's different now." Listening to that person talking about himself, I heard, "I still think the same things that I used to think, but what I do about them is different now." What we learned through the trial was that we can still be family, still love and support each other, even when we have strong and unchanged differences.

When you find your church in the middle of conflict, remember to look for the ways God may be using the conflict to work in your hearts. God may bless you with a chance to grow in love, and even to experience what really loving your enemies can be like, that could only happen through this uncomfortable and unpleasant situation.

DIFFERENCES OF STYLE AND GIFTS ARE GOOD.

The Scripture lets us know that differences of style and gifts are a good thing. The work of the church needs many different kinds of people: organized and spontaneous, sensitive and assertive, detail-oriented people and big-picture thinkers, introverts and extroverts, artists and financial folks. Paul talks about the different parts of the body all being needed and working together in a way that shows that he too might have encountered conflicts between people with different gifts in his churches.

Our different gifts within the church are there to be taken advantage of rather than fought over. You may find that this is also an idea with which it is much easier to agree in theory, but much harder when you are deeply engaged in trying to work with someone who drives you crazy.

One illustration I sometimes use to show working with different styles in action is a skit featuring two characters, Oliver Organized and Sally Spontaneous, trying to plan a dinner together. She is full of ideas about themes, music, decorations, and fun. He just wants to get some specifics tied down, like dates, costs, and who is responsible for what. Their conversation can go one of two ways, either driving them both to screaming frustration or putting together a plan for the evening that uses both of their strengths. The result depends on each person's respect for and willingness to draw on the other person's gifts.

In a small church, you need to use every person's gifts. There aren't any talents that you can afford to waste. The ability to work together because of (rather than in spite of) our differences is more than a theological goal. It is a practical necessity if you are to function as a church.

SIN IS REAL EVEN AMONG US.

The reality is that all of us, even the best of us, in the small church are still sinful human beings. We make mistakes, and sometimes we do nasty or hurtful things to each other on purpose. In a large church, you can simply avoid people you have hurt or who have hurt you. In a small church, you do not have that luxury. The reality of human sin and its consequences is played out every day within the small-church family.

When you are the one sinned against, you know that your enemies will still be in your face. You will see them at worship. They will be at the picnic. Their children will be in the Christmas pageant. They will reach out a hand to you during passing of the peace. You may have to serve them communion or receive communion from their hand. They may know how much they hurt you, or they may not even be aware that there was any harm done.

Let me give you an example. Once, years ago, I wanted to be in charge of the Bible studies in my church. I went up to the woman I knew was looking for someone to do the job, and offered to do it. She never looked at me as I was speaking, and then she turned and walked away. I was deeply hurt and carried that hurt around for months. I learned, long afterwards, that she was so absorbed in her own thoughts that she did not hear a word I said. Yes, she was rude, but she didn't mean to hurt me. She was horrified and apologized immediately when I finally got the courage to mention it.

This is where practicing the advice that Jesus gives in Matthew 18:15–17 is especially important in a small church. Since we are family and need to live together, we need to resolve misunderstanding and hurt as quickly and gently as possible. We are charged to go directly to the person involved and speak to them honestly about what they did, not call several friends on the phone first to get a crowd on our side. The goal is not to be the righteous victim, but to restore the relationship that has been broken by sin.

When you are the one who has sinned, it actually can be more personally painful than having been the victim. While you are still in the same mindset that led to the sin, whether you were tired or angry or jealous or whatever, you felt that what you did was in some way "OK" or justified. Later on, looking at it with a clearer mind, you are more able to see where you were in the wrong. This is a painful thing to see, so we avoid thinking about it, look for ways to blame the other person, or try to rationalize our behavior. When we can think clearly, we tend to be deeply embarrassed by our sin, and we feel for our brother or sister who has been hurt by it.

This is a sad situation to find ourselves in, but there is a prescription in the Scripture. We are called to repent of what we have done, to ask forgiveness of the one we have hurt, and to make restitution for the harm done if it is at all possible. This is our responsibility, whether the other person receives our apology well or poorly. We can only do our share, acknowledge our fault, and try to repair the breach in our relationships. Because we are family, we can hope that the other person will find it in his or her heart to offer forgiveness. Whether or not the person does so becomes one of the challenges in their own spiritual life.

In a small-church family, we play out the human drama of sin, repentance, and forgiveness, over and over, among ourselves. It is part of our own spiritual journey wherever we are, but, in the small church, it is a practical as well as a theological imperative. In a small church, we all need each other, all the time. The consequences of unaddressed sin are too expensive for us to be able to afford.

EVERYONE IS INTERCONNECTED.

A small church lives in and through the relationships of its people, and the impact of events can be felt in the people long after the events have become history. Everyone is interconnected, sometimes in several different ways, and our current relationships are colored by the many different layers of our history. Issues in relationships ripple through the congregation in much the same way that a vibration spreads across a spider web. In a small church, however, the echoes sometimes still can be felt years or even decades later.

Consider the implications of a divorce within a small church. If both spouses are active in the congregation, both have close connections with friends and relatives in the church family. Folks may find themselves in sympathy with one or even both of the partners in conflict. When one partner clearly is behaving badly, this puts a strain on those who have close relationships with that partner. Some will feel they need to be supportive to the misbehaving party out of loyalty, and others will be polarized to the opposite side, taking the misbehavior more personally.

Let me show you the way the ripples of a divorce can spread. One woman I know is a prayer warrior and person of great family loyalty, even though her husband left her in difficult financial circumstances. Although he left the area, he still has family connections in the church. His niece, a church leader, was left conflicted between outrage at her uncle's treatment of his wife and her natural sympathy for him in spite of his faults. This leader's close friend and sister-in-law was also drawn into the conflict because, when the ex-husband needed a place to stay, she provided it for him. The critical incidents happened decades ago, but there are still undercurrents of mistrust and discomfort among the related parties, even now.

In a small church, these complexities in relationships are simply a part of the way things are. They are the material with which the pastor works in bringing the lessons of Scripture home to the reality of daily life in the church. They are also part of the atmosphere—the hidden constraints and obstacles of pastoral ministry. When a pastor sees a hesitation, a small glitch in the expected course of a relationship or a conversation, some strange twist of ancient history may still be having an unexpected impact.

FORGIVING AND FORGETTING HAPPEN IN THE FAMILY.

Learning to forgive and forget is part of life in the small church, because life goes on and we are all in it together. We do learn to live together, through the rocky patches and on into long-term relationships in which we bump along together. If you are part of a small church, you need to build this into your expectations.

I got a glimpse of how this works when I came to my first church. The head deacon gave me an introduction to the board of deacons in which she told me the names of the deacons and gave a brief history of each of them. One deacon couple had a last name I recognized from looking through the church directory, although I had noticed that the family with that name was listed as living several states away. At this point my mind went into slow motion, and it felt as if my thoughts were coated with molasses.

I struggled to put the pieces together. The out-of-state family was the head deacon's son, daughter-in-law, and grandchildren. Her last name was not the same as theirs. The deacon couple had the same last name as the out-of-state family. I was in a fog, but the head deacon just smiled and said, "Oh, yes, he's my ex." It turns out that the head deacon, her ex-husband, and his present wife were all serving as deacons together, and it wasn't a problem.

That last phrase is the key to living together in the small church. Those complicated relationships weren't a problem. The head deacon has had a good marriage and been widowed since her relationship with her fellow deacon, and all the issues between them were in the distant past. The present is the present, and there is work to be done. All three—head deacon, ex, and wife—have caring gifts and serve well as deacons. As grown-ups, they are all able to focus on the present and work together effectively in the caring ministries of the church.

The point is that no matter how difficult or convoluted our past relationships may be, we are still family. When it is time to do the work of the church together, we do it. We may have some of the same kinds of mixed feelings that grown children bring to family reunions, but we are family above all, and we try hard not to let those feelings get in the way of being the church together.

Don't forget that the battle between good and evil and the challenge of learning to love all people, friends and enemies, is not happening somewhere else. It is happening in your own church, among your friends and neighbors, and Jesus is standing beside you, supporting you the whole time.

QUESTIONS FOR REFLECTION AND DISCUSSION

1. How do you feel about conflict? Do you wish you were part of a church without any?

2. Have you thought about conflict as a chance to love your enemies? Does this perspective make a difference?

3. How do you work with people with different backgrounds, political persuasions, theological positions, personality types, and attitudes?

4. How hard is it to recover from a public mistake in your church?

5. Which is harder: forgiving or forgetting?

9

Overcoming Smallness through Shared Ministries

R EMEMBER THAT EVERY CHURCH, and especially a small church, lives
in the wider context of the Christian community. A small church
is not alone. Other churches in its region and other churches in its denomination or association are potential fellow travelers. You do not need
to agree completely with the theology or practices of another group of
Christians to work together in areas where you share concerns. When
your small church sees an opportunity that is too big to handle alone,
sharing it with others is a real possibility.

WE CAN SHARE MUSIC WHEN THERE AREN'T
ENOUGH IN THE CHOIR.

Just because you are in a small church does not mean that you have to
give up forever the kinds of programs that simply need more people. Just
because you have only three or four folks who love to sing and do it well
doesn't mean that they have to give up the hope of singing with a strong
choir and a great music director. I believe that all of those who follow
Jesus and accept him as their Savior are our brothers and sisters. This
especially includes those in other churches in our area. We may disagree
on issues like infant baptism or homosexuality, but we can still sing to the
glory of God together.

One year, an enthusiastic lay leader and one gifted music director put
together a Christmas cantata in our area. Our two or three participants
were joined by those from several other Presbyterian churches in the region for rehearsals during the fall. There were two performances, one on
the south end of the region and one on the north, which were incredibly
beautiful and deeply moving. People from all our small churches had a
chance to hear and to participate in high-quality choral music.

In the county just to the north of us, laypeople from the nine Presbyterian churches meet regularly for what is called the County Connection. Their combined choir is an ongoing activity, providing special concerts at Christmas, Easter, and special events like church anniversaries.

Shared music can also go beyond traditional choir favorites. Another kind of music shared among small churches is praise music, the kind that includes guitars, drums, keyboards, and other instruments. One gifted band in our area is centered between two Presbyterian churches, but includes participants and family members from other churches as well. They have traveled around to the churches in the area to share their music in evening programs of music and prayer. Their willingness to share means that we are all blessed to experience music we do not have the skills and talents to create for ourselves.

In my own church, I have tried to let it be known that we are always open to including whatever special music someone is willing to provide in worship. This can include a child's instrumental as the offertory, a favorite song that a member of the congregation is willing to share, or a piece of music from a friend, a neighbor, or a relative who is passing through. Shared music can be a surprise highlight in the life of a small church.

WE CAN SHARE BIBLE STUDY AND PRAYER.

When my husband and I came to my first pastorate, we had been part of the Alpha program in our previous church. The Presbyterian congregation we came to was not quite ready for Alpha at first, but the people of a nearby Lutheran church were. We introduced them to what we knew about the program and helped them plan and present their first offerings. When it became time to begin the program in our own congregation, they returned the favor.

Our program was on Wednesday nights, while theirs was on Thursdays. We typically offered ours in the fall and winter, while they offered theirs in the fall and spring. We referred people who can not make our schedule to them, and they sent folks who can not fit into their schedule to us. They have invited our people to join in their weekend retreat, which is part of the program. Together, we both had stronger programs than either would have had separately.

The most fun that came out of this cooperation, though, was a Bible study sometimes known as the Alpha alumni group. This was a group of deeply committed Christians from both churches who came together for study of prayer, discernment, faithful life in the workplace, and other topics. The participation of both churches gave this group the critical mass and depth of perspective to act as a practicum in advanced discipleship.

In the same way that two small churches can work together on a program, several churches can bring together an experience that none of them could support individually. Several of our churches in different denominations came together to sponsor a weekend workshop on marriage one year. It included a well-known couple as keynote speakers, discussion groups on a range of topics, a formal dinner, and a worship service that highlighted reaffirmation of wedding vows. Different parts of the program were hosted by different churches. This marriage weekend was a high-quality program—the kind that is often said to be beyond the capability of small churches. None of our churches could have sponsored such a program alone, but together we are able to offer much more.

When you come across an idea that is just what your community needs, do not cross it off your list of possibilities just because it seems to be too big to handle. Your neighboring churches may also feel the potential of the idea, and you may be able to make it work well together.

PASTORS CAN AND SHOULD SUPPORT EACH OTHER.

Being the pastor of a small church can sometimes feel lonely and isolated. You do not have the company of other staff members the way you would in a large church, and some of the concerns you have about your life and work are simply not appropriate to share with members of the congregation. Pastors of other small churches are a good source for mutual caring, support, and encouragement.

Christian pastors ought to be able to support other Christian pastors in spite of our differences of doctrine or politics. I have found that even my colleagues from more conservative denominations, which do not ordain women, have been very supportive of me as a woman pastor. With their willing acceptance of me as a pastor, I am challenged to support those both to the right and to the left of where I stand politically.

Pastoral groups come and go over the years as the life situations and schedules of available participants change. Pastors' lives are very busy, so it takes determination to carve out time for mutual support. A pastors' group does not typically have a large population to draw on, but a base group of six to eight pastors, of which any three make an effective meeting, is usually sufficient.

What do pastors talk about when they get together? Sometimes they simply pray together, or discuss a book, or talk about the Scripture for the coming Sunday. But regardless of the formal topic, the informal conversation can be even more important: This is what is going on in my life; how is life going for you?

Other pastors are the ones who can offer support when an issue comes up in either personal or professional life. These are the ones to offer sympathy when a faction in the church is in rebellion, because they have all been through that experience. These are the ones who can hear your struggles with health issues, doubt, or pure exhaustion, because they have faced them too.

Other pastors are the ones who can help you think through the process of solving problems in ministry. How can I talk with this person who is struggling with addiction? How do I approach this husband who has left his wife and children? How do I deal with a teen whose problem behavior will be a complete surprise to the parents? How do I know when is a good time to introduce a change in the way we do things? Other pastors will not have easy answers, but their experience adds perspective to each struggle. And the knowledge that others appreciate the struggles helps, too.

At one time, I was participating in two different pastor groups. The first was made up of the pastors of other Presbyterian churches in the region, and it met twice each month. There was no formal agenda, but conversation covered a full range of ministry issues. What was particularly helpful was the sharing of information and history about the churches and their people, especially about past events that led people to feel and act the way they do now. Often, each pastor in the conversation understood a piece of the puzzle, and together we were able to come to at least a provisional understanding of what was going on.

The other pastoral group I was participating in was composed of evangelical pastors from several denominations. This group met weekly for an hour and devoted the time pretty strictly to prayer. For me, this was a wonderfully refreshing experience, because I could pray freely without the subconscious assumption that I was somehow the leader: a feeling I have in my own congregation. Simply praising God in prayer with others who are devoting their lives to serving Christ is restorative. I often went back to my own work refreshed and reenergized.

Small-church pastors need to be creative about finding these kinds of sources of support in their own neighborhoods. The relationships and connections made in pastoral groups often lead to cooperation and support in other area of ministry for the churches involved.

CHURCHES CAN SHARE RESOURCES.

There are two formal ways that I know of for sharing resources with people of other small churches. The first happens in conferences dedicated specifically to small-church ministry, often sponsored by denominations or parachurch organizations. The second happens when a large church reaches out to a group of small churches to share the resources it has found or developed.

The Wee Kirk regional conferences sponsored by Presbyterians for Renewal are a good example of programs to support and encourage small churches. These conferences are for lay leaders as well as pastors in small churches, and they provide a chance to get to know others doing the same kinds of ministry and facing the same challenges.

Conference programs typically include well-known speakers who are inspirational as well as motivational and workshops with discussion led by people who are expert in different aspects of ministry. Topics range from deepening prayer life and understanding of Scripture; through practical issues such as mission, worship trends, and youth ministry; to specialized topics such as how to stay healthy as pastors. The regional nature of the conferences allows ideas to be shared and connections to be renewed from year to year.

These conferences and others like them are often staffed by speakers and underwritten by contributions from larger churches as part of their outreach to their smaller companions. Occasionally, a large church acting alone will offer programs for small churches as well. One example of this kind of outreach was a program that the Noroton Presbyterian Church of Darien, Connecticut, offered for the small churches in the Hudson Valley of New York.

One of our small-church pastors had served as an associate at the Noroton church, and he arranged for a Saturday workshop for the deacons of his church and the other small churches in the area. The associate pastor for caring ministries came from Connecticut, and he brought with him several deacons who led different aspects of their caring ministries. Lots of useful ideas flowed in the presentations, and the discussion times helped us figure out how to use those ideas in our own environments.

Different ideas appealed to different participants, of course. For me, the most interesting was a way of keeping track of information about our shut-ins—like interests, food preferences, typical topics of conversation, and preferred times for visits. I also appreciated an approach used to help deacons become more comfortable talking about their faith by sharing the stories of their own faith journeys with each other.

In each area, the presentations gave us a place to start: one approach that had been thought through and tested in practice. We could steal it outright if it would work for us, or we could use the work presented as the basis for starting in our own direction. What works for a large church doesn't necessarily translate to a small church, but learning from large churches does keep us from needing to reinvent things from scratch.

If you are looking for help, look to the larger churches or other organizations that seem to be doing something well. You will often find that a request to share their successful techniques with a group of smaller churches will be received favorably. It is a compliment, after all, to be asked to share what you do well, and showing others how to learn your effective ministry techniques expands the scope of that ministry. Cooperation between large churches and organizations and groups of smaller churches strengthens the ministry of both.

QUESTIONS FOR REFLECTION AND DISCUSSION

1. What do you share with neighboring churches? Music? Bible study? Prayer meetings? Events?
2. How do pastors in the area support each other?
3. Where do you go to meet people from other small churches?
4. What kind of local cooperation would help you most? Could you start it?

10

Making Opportunities for Children and Youth

A SMALL CHURCH USUALLY does not have very many children. Materials designed for children's programs usually assume that the church has a group of children at each age level, and this is not true for a small church. In a small church, you may have only a few children, and those you do have may have very different temperaments or levels of maturity. How do you provide a church home and an experience of faith for children when there are only a few children at a time?

CHILDREN HAVE A PLACE IN WORSHIP.

I am one of those who once believed that children do not belong in worship. They squirm. They drop things. They distract everyone. They drive their parents crazy. And they don't seem to get anything out of the experience, anyway. Particularly with communion, I was of the old school that said you should not be allowed to participate until you could understand what was going on. Then, several young people changed my mind.

The first was a pair of active three-year-olds I met while I was in seminary. They suddenly appeared one Sunday in the pew in front of my regular place. I ached to tell that mother to please get her children under control. During Joys and Concerns, she thanked God for the second anniversary of the adoption of her daughter and for being led to a place where she was welcomed and her children could grow up knowing Jesus. I was ashamed of myself, and I saw those children grow and learn and even be quiet most of the time in worship.

The second was a boy who, in junior high, had a lot of trouble sitting still for my sermons. He would walk back to the entrance area to hang out, and sometimes he would sit in the rocking chair we had back there for babies. In one service, I used as an illustration a missionary poster against the evils of foot-binding in China. He had been hanging out in the rocking chair during the sermon, so I showed him the poster afterward. "Oh, yes," he said, "we learned about that in school." Not only had he heard all that I had said, but he also had some good ideas to add. So much for my thinking that he had not been paying attention.

The third and final set of young people who convinced me that children belong in worship were two very active boys who were about six years old. I was saying the words of institution before communion, when suddenly the words got through to one of the boys. He turned to his mother in sudden tears and said, "Mom, they're going to drink blood!" Suddenly, I found myself including in the liturgy an explanation, first-grade level, of the work of the Holy Spirit who brings into the physical elements the spiritual reality of the presence of Christ. I knew the point had gotten across when the other boy leaned over to his friend when they had their little cups of juice to say, "See, God's in the juice."

We promise, when we baptize babies, to raise our children to be part of the family of Christ. Letting them participate, at whatever level they are able, in the worship life of the church is an important part of keeping this promise. Yes, small children shouldn't have to sit through the long talking of a sermon, but there is no reason that they can't put up with some experiences that they haven't yet come to understand.

Every worship service should have a time for children, if any are present. If the pastor is not comfortable leading children's time, any member of the church family, especially a grandmother or grandfather, can lead it. One pastor friend of mine uses the children's time to tell an Old Testament story from the lectionary. Others use "show and tell" objects, like a stapler to remind us how God's love holds us together. I like to ask a lot of questions, hopefully to evoke the answer that is the main point of the sermon to come—such as the idea that God goes with us on summer vacation because God is always here for us.

Children should also be included in leading worship from time to time. For one church, this means the annual service at the end of the Sunday School year in June. The older children help design the service, listening to the lectionary Scripture and deciding on the sermon topic and main points. They build the liturgy, choosing prayers and music, and then lead the prayers and readings. During the service, younger children greet and hand out bulletins, collect the offering, and lead some of their favorite songs. I have even seen teens break the bread and pour the cup at the communion table. Children and teens become participants and rather than simply audience in a service led by young people.

A time that includes children should be an expected part of worship. You can find many resources to use for children's time in worship: read-aloud Bible stories, books of object sermons, children's messages tied to the lectionary, etc. Your leader can be anyone who likes children and who is willing to put up with the unexpected. With time for children in worship, you give the congregation a chance to get to know its children as well as show all the grown-ups that worship has a place for everyone. You also make for the children a place in worship where they feel at home in the church family.

CHILDREN AND YOUTH CAN PARTICIPATE IN ADULT MINISTRIES.

The involvement of children begins in worship and then extends outward into all the activities of the church. It should be possible for you to find ways to integrate children and youth into most of the adult ministries of the small church.

Children can become an important part of the special events of the church seasons. They make the centerpieces and special decorations for celebrations like Christmas and Mother's Day. One year, it was the teens who decorated the sanctuary with lilies for Easter. When there are special lunches or dinners, it is especially nice to have the teens behind the table as hosts and servers. The point is that, whenever we gather for fellowship, the children should not only be welcome to participate, but also be included among the many hands that make it happen.

One church typically has one or two young people, usually of high school age, who serve on the board of deacons. They are fully responsible deacons, participating in meetings, sharing responsibility for coffee hour, serving communion, and helping in the caring ministries. As they grow into adult capabilities (and receive their drivers' licenses), the junior deacons are very helpful wherever and whenever a need arises.

It is important that you let young people know they are welcome wherever their interests lead them to show up, whether it is to sing in the choir, deliver clothing for the homeless, join in the discussion at Bible study, run a refreshment stand at the yard sale, or just hang out and chat during coffee hour. Children and youth are members of the church family, and including them in all the ways the family works together should be normal and expected.

YOUTH BECOME LEADERS AND MODELS FOR YOUNGER CHILDREN.

It is important even, and perhaps especially, when there are few children, to have an expected progression into positions of more responsibility and the privileges that go with that progression. Something was lost, for example, when the youngest baseball players got their Little League uniforms—you no longer had to work and wait to get the privileges that were for the "big kids."

In the small church, when older youth and teens have their own responsibilities, they should have the benefits to go with them. These benefits might be an amusement park trip, travel to a youth conference, or a time of visibly being in charge. Often, the young people will decide for themselves what they would like to have for their privileges of rank, and the adults around them only need to discern what these are and figure out how to make them happen.

One small church holds a communicants' class every two or three years, and all of those of junior high age or older are welcome. In one class, there were four students, and then two of the boys from the previous group also joined as teaching assistants. It is wonderful to see these bright and caring young people encourage each other as they face the moral and ethical challenges around them—issues of sex, drugs, smoking, prejudice, and gang violence, to name a few.

SOCIAL EVENTS ARE FOR BRINGING FRIENDS.

One year, the church I served finally realized that an important role in the Sunday School was "events coordinator," and we looked for a volunteer for that particular job. Usually, the responsibility for the children's special events had fallen on the Sunday School superintendent and teachers, and the additional workload just didn't seem fair.

This Sunday School sponsors five different events each year for the church family and other children who are related to the church. There are two breakfasts for the whole church: one on rally day to kick off the school year and the other at the end of Sunday School. The other three are seasonal celebrations: the Harvest Festival (specifically not Halloween, although costumes are welcome), the children's Christmas party on the day of the pageant, and the Easter Egg Hunt.

The two breakfasts are times when the children and their teachers host the adults, and the adults come to meet and support the children's programs. They are also times to talk about programs planned for and work done during the Sunday School year.

The children's fellowship celebrations are something more, and over the years they have developed a life of their own. These are times when friends, neighbors, and relatives of those in the church family bring their children. These events may have triple, or even six times, the number of children who attend Sunday School, and, with other family members, there may be more people at the event than on a busy Sunday in church.

Why are these social events important and worth all the effort? They are opportunities for our friends and neighbors to spend time in the church, to get to know us and each other, and to feel comfortable in the church environment. When you make the church a welcoming setting for regular celebrations, perhaps it will not be so hard for those who face a crisis, or who simply want to know more about God, to find comfort there.

REGIONAL YOUTH ACTIVITIES CONNECT WITH PEERS.

When you only have half a dozen or so teens in your church, each with his or her own schedule of activities and athletics, it is not easy to have a full-scale youth program. On the other hand, when there are only a few teens who share Christian values, they need to spend time with others with a similar mindset. The solution to this dilemma can sometimes be found in regional or denominational youth programs.

One example of this kind of program is Nightwatch, an event for youth and their leaders held at the Cathedral of St. John the Divine in New York City. The cathedral opens itself to groups of youth from all over the country, and it provides fellowship, music, and worship, as well as a place to sleep overnight on the floor in the gym. One program I attended involved about two hundred people from the ninety churches of our presbytery. Some churches had groups of a dozen or more, but others were similar to our delegation of three teens and one adult. Large groups and small groups were all welcomed enthusiastically.

For our folks, it was a great experience. Even coming in, into that mass of teens, there were already some friends. We were mixed up into groups and introduced to new faces. There was a scavenger hunt to learn about the magnificent sanctuary, and we all wandered our way around a labyrinth. Our small group became part of a larger "we," and we could feel that as a small church we were not alone in the body of Christ.

This kind of experience is critically important for our small-church youth, because it is easy to think that what we see in our own church is all that there is of the church. Regional gatherings, whether conferences, summer camps, workshops, or overnight adventures, ground us in the wider church and help us all to know that we in the small church are not alone. When you look, you will find a surprising variety of possibilities to connect your own young people to the experience of the wider church.

QUESTIONS FOR REFLECTION AND DISCUSSION

1. How do you provide worship experiences for children? What compromises have you made to include children?

2. How do young people grow into doing the work of the church?

3. What opportunities do you have for older children to practice leadership?

4. How do you engage friends and neighborhood children in church events?

5. What regional and national opportunities are there that your children and youth could experience?

11

Technological Tools in the Small Church

TECHNOLOGY CAN BE HELPFUL.

PERSONAL COMPUTERS AND RELATED equipment can help a small church do many of the same things a large church does, from educational materials and record keeping to publicity. However, interest and skills in technology are spotty and can pop up in the most unexpected places. While many small-church folks may not like computers, often grandparents or even great-grandparents keep in touch with family through email. Usually, there are one or two people who just plain enjoy gadgets and so keep up with the latest technology. Often, there is a cluster of people who enjoy passing on the latest jokes and urban legends around by email. There may also be one or two people who learned to use spreadsheets on the job and can help set them up for the church.

I read a sign once that said, "You can have it good, or you can have it quick, or you can have it cheap. Pick any two." For the small church, in order to get things both good and cheap, it takes a little more time. For example, I have a wonderful low-cost printer that does very high quality photograph printing; the only hitch is that it takes a long time to print a picture. This kind of trade-off works for me because, although I want good quality pictures, I don't want them very often or want very many of them at a time.

The most useful tools I know are:

Copiers: We all use them for the Sunday bulletin and the newsletter, but they can do a whole lot more. With fancy paper folded to greeting-card size and matching envelopes, we can make very nice personalized cards and invitations. Folding a sheet in thirds makes a good brochure that can also be mailed. Using photo quality copying and zoom to adjust sizes, along with scissors and tape, we can make and multiply just about anything we need.

Word processing: Even for the slowest, least accurate typist (the one I see in the mirror), a word processor makes it possible to capture what you want to say on paper. The key is to use only those features, out of the many offered, that you actually need. Reusing a previous document makes it possible to have a consistent format for bulletins, newsletters, agendas, minutes, announcements, and educational materials.

Spreadsheets: Because spreadsheets do calculations and change totals whenever a line changes, they can save a lot of the headaches for financial people, and especially financial volunteers. Annual reports, monthly financials, and budgets become much easier and more professional with a spreadsheet to provide the organization of the numbers and to do the calculating and balancing. Once an "expert" has set up the pattern, the week-to-week work of managing money becomes much cleaner.

Email: Messages with announcements and prayer requests are more reliable through email than our telephone tree used to be. Capturing the joys and concerns on Sunday and circulating them by email saves deciphering the notes taken on the backs of bulletins and ensures that all the prayer warriors are informed of critical issues in time. Distributing meeting minutes and agendas by email helps make it more likely that we are all on the same page at meeting time. If at least half of a group has email access, each non-technological person can be matched to a partner who will pass things on to them.

Internet: Almost anything the church could want or need is available and comparable online, from furniture and office supplies to reference materials of all kinds. You can even order background checks for potential volunteers, to make sure that the person with the bad driving record isn't doing transportation for children or the one coming back from credit problems isn't counting the collection.

Web sites: Having a Web site for your church is a way to make it visible to those who are comfortable using the Internet, the same way the church building is visible to those who drive by. A simple site with information about services and events lets people know what is happening. Pictures of the building (so visitors know what to look for), the pastor and leaders (so they can be recognized), and some people in the midst of regular activities (to give a feel for the atmosphere) are also helpful. The first goal of a site is to invite folks to experience the real thing, so it does not need to be elaborate or sophisticated, but simply reflect the style of your church family.

Scanning and digital photography: Pictures of the congregation busy at the work of the church are always helpful—to remind us of what we are doing and why we are doing it, and to inspire us to imagine what we might be doing differently or better. We also just like looking at family pictures. Pictures actually reinforce our relationships and continue our connectedness by including those who weren't there at the time.

OCR (optical character recognition) scanning allows us to use quotations and text from many sources as we build our sermons, presentations, and educational materials. It is also a way to get research materials into a place and form where they can be more easily found and used when they are become relevant.

TECHNOLOGY IS ABOUT COMMUNICATION.

Technology is not of value for its own sake, but only if it communicates the message of the gospel and facilitates the life and work of the God's people. Technology is about finding the information we need, storing it until we need it, and presenting it to the right people, at the right time, and in a form that can be received and understood.

What kinds of information do you work with in the small church? There is scriptural and theological content that reflects the gospel message—the ideas upon which sermons, educational materials, and outreach materials are based. There is news about the work and activities of the church shared within the church family and to the wider community. There are the specific details of that work shared as the work is being done—things like schedules, agendas, requests, and minutes. There is also the view into the church's life, which you provide for your neighbors through invitations, publicity, and church Web sites.

Large numbers of resources for education and for biblical research are available on the market. The range of books alone can be overwhelming. One summer, as we prepared for a study of the Gospel of John in the fall, we ordered only a few samples of the dozens of available study guides to choose from. There are books about accounting systems for churches, books dealing with bereavement, books on identifying spiritual gifts, books about puppetry for children, books describing mission opportunities all over the world, and books on how to run programs of all kinds. The quandary for the small church is more which opportunities to take advantage of, rather than specifically how to approach any particular problem.

In a small church, you do not need to find speakers or create materials to have an education program that is both broad and deep. Even beyond the available books, many programs are available in video form with discussion guides. A sampling of the video curricula on my bookshelf includes basics of faith, evangelism programs, drama from the history of the church, scriptural approaches to mental and spiritual health, worship alternatives, practical prayer ministry, and church leader training. Many more options are available at a reasonable price when we are done with these topics.

Bible software and biblical research tools provide a small-church pastor and interested lay folks with tools that were once available only to those near a seminary library. The small laptop on which I am typing this holds the full thirty-eight volumes of the *Early Church Fathers,* more than a dozen Bible translations, the Hebrew and Greek Scriptures with several lexicons each, the full set of Calvin's commentaries and several others, an archeological encyclopedia of the Holy Land with maps, and a variety of theological references. All can be searched for words or phrases to make the references for a particular topic instantly available. Pastors and scholars of even a generation ago could not have imagined the information available to leaders in the most isolated small church.

A small church no longer needs to be an isolated church. Technology gives us all access to such a rich variety of options for Bible study, program offerings, and practical advice on how to do what we are called to do. You may have trouble finding exactly what you are looking for in the mass of material available, but you will not be left without resources and ideas in just about every aspect of church life.

MUSIC CAN BE A CHALLENGE.

Providing quality music can be a challenge in the small church, as fewer music students are learning to play our beautiful organs and our small numbers may or may not include some folks with musical gifts. In five and a half years in one small church, I never had a regular organist or choir director. This was not for lack of searching; we simply could not find someone near enough to commit to the job.

We were blessed that, in those same years, we had several people who were willing to play either the organ or piano, or both, nearly every Sunday. Our music came from one organist who retired years ago (but still comes back sometimes), a college freshman who learned to play for his home church, a college music major who plays on his vacations, and our Sunday School pianist who is willing to fill in sometimes. Only once or twice over the years have I come to the end of the week with no coverage for worship music.

But what do you do, on those days in a small church, when there is no one to provide music? I know of two alternatives, neither perfect, but both of which work. The first option is recorded music, either from regular performances, special accompaniment recordings, or recordings made by someone in the church in advance.

The second option is a piece of technology called a "digital hymnal." This is actually a computer, too, about the size of a laptop, programmed with the tunes from a dozen or more hymnals. The company that makes the one I have is also expert at synthesizing instruments, so the device has options for many types of instruments and combinations. What you do is choose the hymns you want to use, choose the instrumentation, and then either use the little speakers on the box or plug it into the church sound system. You then cue the songs during the service with a remote control. The sound is a bit mechanical because it is a computer playing rather than a human, but with this kind of machine, there is never a day without music.

QUESTIONS FOR REFLECTION AND DISCUSSION

1. What tools or resources does your church use? Who are your experts?

2. What more tools do you wish you had? What other technology do you think might help?

3. How can you be creative with what you already have?

4. When you identify resources that would help, do you remember to pray for your church's needs?

5. Where can you go for donations and expert advice?

PART III

The Pastoral Role in the Small Church

12

What Small Churches Need from Their Pastors

WHAT KINDS OF THINGS SHOULD A PASTOR DO?

IN A LARGE CHURCH with a professional staff, a person sitting in worship can assume that a lot of the work of the church is handled by the professionals who know their business. The professionals are usually very good at the various tasks of ministry, and, after all, that's what they're paid to do. The people in the pews on Sunday morning can also assume that they have made their contribution to the work of the church when they put their offering into the plate each week. One might feel like the family's share of the church's ministry has been taken care of with a check, especially if the check is a generous one.

In the small church, everyone can see clearly and painfully that there is not enough money to pay someone to do all the ministry that needs to be done. It is necessary for everybody to be involved in ministry, and this causes a shift in the way small-church members see their professional staff. They can more easily see that the pastor's job is not just to do ministry for them, but to help them do ministry for themselves.

I recently asked a Bible study group of about a dozen people from two different active small churches what they expect a pastor to do for their church. In the list they made, there was a very interesting mix of tasks, both doing ministry directly and helping others to do ministry. Here are some of the "jobs" of the pastor that they listed:

- Conduct worship
- Do weddings, baptisms, and funerals
- Preach a biblical message
- Encourage self-sufficiency of the congregation (help members learn to preach and lead worship)

- Oversee education for adults and children
- Encourage spiritual growth
- Encourage reading Scripture
- Know people's gifts/strengths and know ministry needs
- Match gifts to needs
- Incite evangelism
- Facilitate leadership, evangelism, and mission
- Lead in intercession and encourage healing prayer and practices
- Delegate administration, building issues, etc.
- Visit the sick and shut-in
- Know what's going on
- Provide counseling and referral for problems
- Be holy personally—take time to read and pray
- Pray for the people
- Invite the Holy Spirit into the community
- Be an example in life and marriage
- Show a life commitment to the church

For this group of active small-church members, the work of overseeing, delegating, encouraging, and facilitating appeared in every area of ministry, even including preaching and leading worship. The idea of congregational self-sufficiency was important to folks from both churches in our group. On one hand, self-sufficiency means that the church is not dependent on the pastor to be open for worship on Sunday—for example, in cases of illness, vacation, or other crises. On the other hand, being self-sufficient means that experienced Christians are confident and able to step in to lead the worship and to create and deliver sermons, often from their own perspective and including their own personal testimony of faith.

Different groups in different churches will have somewhat different emphases in expressing these various roles of the pastor, but the sense that the pastor encourages participation is consistent across active small churches. In one case I know, when an interim followed a "do everything for the people" pastor, one congregant said, "He was the best thing that ever happened to us. He refused to do anything for us, and we learned to do things for ourselves." In another situation, a pastor said, "My heart attack was one of the best things that happened to this church, because it showed people that they could handle things, and that everything didn't depend on me."

You may feel that the better and more complete job of ministry the pastor can do, the better off the church will be, but this is not the way it is. The best job your pastor can do is to strengthen the ministries of the people so that the church is not dependent on the pastor's own personal ministry. As a small church, you will sometimes be without a pastor; if your pastor has done a good job, you will still be a church.

PASTORS MUST LOVE THE PEOPLE.

When Jesus said that the two greatest commandments were to love God and to love others, he wasn't kidding. Jesus lived out his love for the Father and for the people around him every day. The pastor of a small church represents Jesus, directly and personally, to the people of the church and the community. Empathy, compassion, and love must underlie the pastor's every action and relationship.

In a small church, the pastor must have a connection with and be an advocate for every individual in his or her care. One of my predecessors told the story of counseling with both halves of a couple going through a divorce. When one of the partners challenged her, asking, "Whose side are you on, anyway?" she replied, "Whomever I'm talking to at the time." She was exactly correct. A pastor must advocate for the best interests of every individual that he or she counsels, even when those people are in direct conflict with each other.

Because a small church lives in and through relationships, the pastor must have a relationship with each person in the church family, and that relationship needs to be perceptibly loving for the person on the receiving end. All of the people need to know, on the basis of their own direct personal experience, that the pastor cares about them and has their best interests at heart.

This is one way that a small church is very different from a large or medium-sized church. Gary McIntosh, in the book *One Size Doesn't Fit All,* compares the reactions of the people of small and medium sized churches to their pastors. Where the people of a larger church care about the pastor's abilities and skills and performance, the small church is in a different place.[1]

COMMENTS ABOUT A SUCCESSFUL PASTOR IN A SMALL CHURCH	COMMENTS ABOUT A SUCCESSFUL PASTOR IN A MEDIUM CHURCH
Our minister loves everyone!	Our pastor is an organizer.
He's such a warm and kindhearted person that we all love him.	Our pastor is one of the most creative people I've known.
He cares for us and knows us by name.	The pastor has put together a good team.
Everyone in the community respects him.	He's well prepared for every meeting.
He treats everyone the same.	He's a great planner.
He's got a real sense of humor.	He's a superb preacher.
The kids all like him.	He's a good teacher.

Conversely, whatever may be in their hearts, if pastors in small churches are perceived as distant or unemotional, they will have difficulty bonding with the people, which is critical to being accepted in a pastoral relationship in the small church.

If you are serving as a small-church pastor, you may find this reality painful. You may love the people deeply, but have trouble showing it. You may care about the struggles you see in each one and pray for their good with your whole heart, but at the same time struggle yourself with expressing the way you feel to the people directly. Finding a way to move the love from your heart out to your smile and your voice is important, especially for the people of a small church.

PASTORS HAVE TO BE THERE WHEN THEY'RE NEEDED.

The single biggest cause of conflicts I have seen between the people of a small church and their pastors is the sense among the people that the pastor has not been there for them when they needed it. Members of the congregation feel this personally as a serious betrayal of trust, and it can be very, very hard to heal.

1. McIntosh, *One Size Doesn't Fit All*, 61–62.

One pastor I know is still puzzled by the loss of a critical, deep friendship with a couple in his congregation. He remembers many times when he supported both members of the couple, and many good times that he and his wife shared with them. He never really understood why their relationship cooled and the couple left the church.

From the couple's side, what happened was an "unforgivable" breach. The husband had been in a traffic accident quite late at night. He had killed a pedestrian whom he had not seen at all. It turned out to be likely that the pedestrian had intentionally been hard to see, intending to commit suicide. The couple called the pastor out of bed, and he spent an extended time on the phone with the husband, but he did not come to their house. The pastor had been exhausted after a long and difficult day. He felt that he could not do more, so he did not go. This particular couple felt betrayed by his absence, abandoned when he did not make the effort to come to them in their need. The couple simply could not believe or accept that he would choose not to be with them at this most difficult time in their lives. The pastor never knew how important that moment had been to his people, and they never told him.

Of course, from the pastor's point of view, the key to being there when you're needed is to be able to tell when that critical moment is. Sometimes people will tell you what they need, and sometimes they won't, assuming that if you "really cared" you would know automatically. Sometime your pressing into a situation is perceived as caring, and sometimes it's seen as intrusive. As a pastor, you are supposed to know the people so well that you are able to guess right about which situations demand an immediate presence and which can wait for the next day.

At one point, I had two members of my congregation who were dying of cancer at the same time. One was an intensely private person who reluctantly permitted a brief visit in the hospital. The most I could do to help her was to make sure that another pastor who was a close friend was available for her. With the other, I could be personally present through the various twists and turns of the disease and serve the needs of the family as best I understood them.

"He wasn't there!" or "She didn't come" are the most poignant and deeply emotional cries of small-church members who feel let down by their pastor. As pastor, you may have a dozen good reasons why you couldn't be there. These good reasons make no difference to the parishioner with a broken heart. In a small church, where you are a critical part of each person's life, discerning those times when you simply must be there is a crucial part of the ability to do ministry. And, since you are human too, you will make mistakes.

PASTORS MUST BE WILLING TO BE LOVED BACK.

Pastors are giving people, and as Christians we have been taught from childhood that it is more blessed to give than to receive. Often, pastors and lay leaders share the conviction that it is just not appropriate to be on the receiving end of a gift. In the small church, this conviction gets in the way of relationships, because, for the long term, all relationships need to be balanced.

This does not mean that a pastor can "use" his or her congregation to meet personal needs for love, or affirmation, or whatever. For personal support, a pastor must look to family and friendships outside of the immediate church environment.

This also does not mean that a pastor is free to participate emotionally in the lives of the people who come for help. A person can easily become attached to a pastor who listens with care for the first time in a lifetime, and the pastor must be careful to keep clear boundaries, especially if the person is of the opposite sex.

What it does mean is that a pastor must be open to being emotionally engaged with the people in ways that are mutual, trusting, and affectionate. When the pastor is doing a good job, the people will react positively and personally. They respond with affection for pastoral care, relief when a difficult situation is resolved, gratitude for forgiveness when they have been wrong, and so forth. They will want to express their feelings, and they will try to "give back" some of what they feel they have received.

Pastors need to make provisions that allow their people to express these feelings in effective ways. If you are the pastor, you need to let the people know what you consider a "treat." Special favors may be as simple as being asked to dinner at home, or going together to a restaurant, or having a favorite pastry at coffee hour, or wearing hand-knit sweaters, or going to a concert or a show, or having a special plant to put in the garden, or trying a new wine. Preferences in this area are completely personal, and pastors need to be open about what gives them joy so that, when someone wants to make them happy, that person will know what to do.

If you are doing your job as a small-church pastor, you will make people happy from time to time, and it is especially nice if there are ways for people to return the favor. As pastors, we do not usually think of enjoying the gifts of others as part of our ministry; but receiving as well as giving is an important part of our pastoral relationships. So, pastors, simply relax and enjoy.

PREACHING TAKES AN EDUCATED BACKGROUND AND REALISTIC APPLICATIONS.

Each pastor and seminary student comes to his or her own understanding of how to prepare for a sermon, and this is the part of a pastor's job that is usually well supported by our education. I find that simplicity is best for me, since, in the busyness and complications of the average week, I need to be able to focus Sunday's message clearly.

My particular approach to sermon constructions has four elements—some sort of engagement in the topic (a question, an anecdote, a paradox, imagining the Scripture situation, etc.), the content and meaning of the underlying Scripture passage, the connections and implications of the passage for our community today, and a challenge for applying the topic in real situations. I believe in asking the Holy Spirit to help me capture the message in manuscript so that, wherever my head may be on Sunday morning, at least the words will be available to the people. I do not want my personal ego or nervousness to come between the message and those who are there to hear it.

One of the best ideas I heard in seminary was to have an imaginary council to listen as you try out parts of the sermon in your mind in order to see how council members might react. The members of the council represent folks who are listening from different perspectives. What you say to appeal to a person of emotional faith, for instance, needs to be tried from the perspective of a more analytical listener, and what you put in to appeal to a teen should also make sense to an older person. There are many perspectives in a small church, and it is important that the sermon message include aspects that are accessible to each of them.

Preaching the word begins with an accurate understanding of Scripture, and each pastor must engage with it honestly and try to understand what God has to say in those words. This means doing the work of analysis and research: investigating the context and uncovering the meaning based on the intent of the writer. We must not get "lazy" when we leave school behind and assume that we get the point because the message we think we hear matches our personal opinions or political priorities.

As we prepare our sermons, it is important that we present our messages in the context of a balanced doctrine, carefully thinking through the theological implications of what we hear and what we plan to say. Our people may never have heard the word "Pelagian" (and never want to), but it is up to us to understand and explain the implications of the relationship between works and grace. Solid theology is the foundation for preaching, even if it never shows up in the words themselves.

In a small church, practical illustrations and practical implications are crucial in our preaching. Theology and Scripture are not for special occasions, to be taken out and used only for special events. They are intensely practical, to be applied as we are heading home from church, as we relax on Sunday afternoon, while we do our work during the week, and while we socialize with our friends. Each person who listens on Sunday morning should find some direct application of the message in his or her own life during the week. If you are the pastor, your job is to make the link between the biblical word and the lived experience of your people.

PASTORAL INTEGRITY MEANS LIVING BY WHAT YOU PROFESS.

The pastor of a small church is *always* visible, both to the people of the church and to the people of the wider community. Strangely enough, pastors of larger churches with more people observing them actually may be able to have more private lives outside of the scrutiny of others, but small-church pastors do not have this luxury. Even though we know that all secrets will be revealed on the day of judgment, in a small church even the best-kept secrets are usually revealed much sooner.

The small-church pastor represents the church family, and the people have a vested interest in making sure that their representative looks good. As a pastor, the way you dress, the way you drive, the bad word you said when you lost your temper, the political meeting you went to, the people you were seen lunching with, the causes you contribute to, and hundreds of other details of your life are all open to the public. You may not like it, but this is the way it is in a small church.

There is a story about a driver who was pulled over by police after some particularly rude, but not illegal, driving. The driver was noisy and irate, protesting that he hadn't broken any laws. The officer replied that he thought the car had been stolen, since the driver's style was so different from the Christian bumper stickers on the car. Being a small-church pastor is like wearing a bumper sticker on your forehead, and everything you do is compared with and attributed to the Lord you represent.

There is another story that I like, which easily could be urban legend. A pastor hurried to the grocery store at a busy time for just a few things. After waiting through a long line, he paid for his purchases with a ten-dollar bill. Getting to the car, he found that he had received an extra ten in change. He went back and waited through the line again and said to the cashier, "I think there's been a mistake. You gave me too much change." The cashier said, "There's no mistake. I know who you are. I was in your church last week, so I know what kind of preacher you are. I wanted to see what kind of man you are." If you are a pastor, your life is public all the time.

Integrity in the pastorate means living by what you profess. It means doing your best to do the right thing. It also means not hiding your messes and pretending that you're better than you really are. It means living transparently: repenting of your own sins and making restitution as publicly as you do everything else. Don't ever think people won't notice what you do, and don't ever let go of the fact that who you are reflects either well or poorly on the Lord you serve.

QUESTIONS FOR REFLECTION AND DISCUSSION

1. How does your church care for its pastor?
2. What does your church need most from your pastor?
3. How do you show your appreciation?
4. How do you communicate feedback and suggestions to your pastor?
5. How do you react when your pastor makes a mistake or fails in some part of the job?

13

What Life Is Like for a Small-Church Pastor

SOME THINGS ARE PREDICTABLE.

THE FIRST THING I noticed about life as a small-church pastor is how unstructured the work is. Other than Sundays, which come around regularly, and the seasons of the church year, there is no obvious way to choose what to do next at any given moment. Even when I was an entrepreneur starting my own company, the work organized itself by priority and other people's schedules. In seminary, there were classes and meetings, with lots of small assignments due soon and a few big assignments due later which needed to be done in stages. Small-church pastors have more things to do than they can possibly complete, but what order to do them in is not at all obvious.

Of course, some things are predictable. Next Sunday morning is coming, whether we are thinking about it or not. The holidays come every year, with all their traditional accoutrements. Since small churches live by the seasons, and since what we do this year is rooted in what we did last year, we can sense that any particular day is some part of the annual cycle. However, this sense of time doesn't answer the question of what I as a pastor choose to do this morning versus this afternoon or next week.

I found that it was not possible for me to "get ahead" of the weekly cycle. I do create a preaching calendar with the Scripture passages that will be the focus of each week's sermon covering several months at a time, but I can not be involved with more than one set of Scripture at a time. This means that when one Sunday service is over, I put away that set of thoughts and bring out the next Scripture to hold in mind for the next several days. I make that Scripture the center of my devotions and thoughts, as well as the grounds for my research, planning, and writing.

Usually, by the end of the week, the Holy Spirit has "cooked" my understanding of what that Scripture means for this particular group of people this week, and a sermon emerges.

There are other things that appear on my to-do list regularly, every week. The worship service liturgy comes about relatively early in the week as a side effect of early meditation on the passage readings. The children's message ideas come after the main concepts of the sermon are clear, and it is usually the result of interaction of those ideas with the experiences of daily life. Preparation for adult studies, when I am leading them on Wednesday and/or Sunday, happens in office times during the week when that work is not superseded by emergencies.

My week as a pastor built itself into a rhythm: Mondays for office preparation, phone calls, and evening meetings; Tuesdays for prayer group, denominational meetings, and visiting; Wednesdays for writing and program preparation; Thursdays for education and reading; Fridays for family; Saturdays for church and community events. This is the background theme music against which the daily drama of the unexpected and unpredictable unfolds.

I offer this pattern of time not as a recommendation, but as an example of one way to structure the unstructured work of parish ministry. I am not a particularly organized or disciplined person, and I can use up more time deciding what to do next than it takes to do the next task itself. It helps me to be able to think, as I get up in the morning, "It's Monday—what follow-up calls do I have to make and what office work is waiting in line?" or "It's Tuesday—whom do I need to see?" Each pastor has to decide how to structure the flow of work as suits the ability to be productive, but I suggest thinking about finding a particular structure that feels comfortable.

Instead of holding office hours, I used to open the sanctuary of the church most evenings at dinnertime. I put out an "open" sign, and everyone knew that it was a time they could usually find me. The hour between six and seven in the evening is a time when workers are on their way home, teens are out of school, and retirees often have had dinner. It is a space before those who have evening meetings need to be at them. I was always open to appointments whenever, but I found that most folks like to just drop in. Unstructured time in the church with the lights on lets the time be used for whatever the visitor needs.

You can see seasonal events coming, and, as a pastor, you know that you need to be getting ready for them slightly before anyone else notices them. I think of those distant events as like icebergs: The part you can see coming is really part of a much larger thing that is much closer, but hidden under the water. The big, hidden part is the preparation that needs to be done before the visible event gets here. Thinking of an event as like an iceberg makes me just nervous enough, just early enough, to actually get the preparation done by the time it is needed. You will need to have your own way of building the awareness of coming events into your own time allocation process.

SOME THINGS ARE UNPREDICTABLE.

While the predictable work of pastoring gives an underlying rhythm to daily life, much of a pastor's work is unpredictable, coming out of the circumstances and events of the people's lives. Once, I returned from two days away at Christmastime to find that one elder had had a serious stroke and one Sunday School teacher's cousin and closest friend had died suddenly. Another night, as I came to open the sanctuary, I found waiting for me a nurse whose private patient had asked to be taken off life support and wanted her to be there with him. Yet again, one Sunday evening, just as I was relaxing for bed, an older teen who had just been raped showed up at my door. You can never tell what will happen next, and the pastor is the first line of defense for many of the people of a small church in times of crisis.

As a pastor, you are never ready for these things, but a pastor must always be ready for these kinds of things. I once took a class in disaster preparedness given by the Salvation Army, and one speaker, a veteran of several disasters, said, "The most important thing is to stay prayed-up." We pastors can never have the wisdom, the strength, the compassion, or even the raw energy to do what we need to do, without the power of God behind us. We have to keep our relationship with God alive and current, so that when the unexpected moment comes, we know where to find the strength we need.

When the two women of my congregation were dying of cancer at the same time, one wanted to withdraw to her family while the other wanted to be engaged with her many friends. The first did not want much visiting, but the second I saw nearly every day, and sometimes more often than that. When folks from the congregation had been visiting her, they often needed to stop by my place to chat as well. These needs for support simply became the highest priority at the moment, regardless of what other things might have been on the schedule.

Like many small-church pastors, I am not trained as a psychologist, so most of my responses to personal crises involve a lot of listening and then making referrals to the experts. I have found that, most of the time, the person in crisis is the one who actually knows best what kind of help he or she needs. Typically, the pastor only needs to let that person think things through out loud in order to figure out what to do. I keep files of community resources of all kinds, and I have been carefully collecting the phone numbers for different kinds of crisis lines, hoping never to need them.

One part of our traditional pastor's role comes with its own timing: the major life transitions of baptism, confirmation, marriage, and funeral. When the need arises, we simply make room for them in our schedules and in the life of the church. These events take some time and preparation for the worship services, but they usually also include time behind the scenes and time for conversation and counseling. These are particularly important times when our consciousness of God's presence can break into everyday life with a special brightness and poignancy. Part of the pastor's role is to point out and help make sense of the many feelings involved in these transition points.

If you are a small-church pastor, you know that the telephone or the doorbell can ring at any time of day or night. As a pastor, you need to be ready for absolutely anything to happen next.

THE PASTOR PROVIDES A CONTEXT FOR ACTION.

Pastors provide the scriptural and theological context for the activities of the church through their preaching and teaching. In a small church, the pastor is the one who reminds the people that what they do as a church is the work of Christ in the world, that what they are really doing is bringing of the presence of the kingdom of God into their neighborhood.

This should not mean that the pastor gives a lot of direct instructions to the congregation about what projects to support, which causes to join, or what candidates to vote for in the next election. When I first came to join the church, one of the men in my new-member class had been part of an activist congregation. He said, "I don't want someone to tell me what to do. I want someone to tell me what the Scripture says, and then I'll decide what God wants me to do about it." He was exactly right. The pastor's job is to provide the background against which specific decisions of what to do and not to do can be made.

The pastor's job is to explain the Scripture in sermons, hopefully provide illustrations that make the ideas presented clear and relevant, and then challenge the people to act on what they have heard. When there are Bible studies and other adult education classes, the pastor can delve into specific areas in more detail and encourage the kind of discussion where participants can become engaged in the ideas. The pastor should be providing the people an understanding of the principles that they apply in daily life and work, both individually and as a church family.

Some of the ways a pastor can engage the people in the work of ministry, within the teaching of the gospel, are:

Renewing a commitment to purpose: The pastor's role, through preaching and teaching as well as informal conversation, is to bring our attention out of the details of how to do what we do, and to help us to consider why we are doing it. The pastor reminds us all of the reasons behind our work, and does it in a way that refreshes our dedication and renews our motivation.

Beginning new ministries: The pastor is one person in a small church who is looking for both commands of Christ and opportunities to respond to those commands in addressing the needs of the world. The pastor can offer suggestions for action and see whether people in the congregation feel called to follow them. The pastor is also the one to help a person who senses a particular calling to explore what the call means, to guide planning, and to help organize the way a new ministry can be established in the church family.

Developing practical evangelism: Encouraging evangelism involves more than a simple, if impassioned, call from the pulpit in a small church. It involves helping folks understand how to notice opportunities, how to listen to others, how to share their own stories, and how to invite others into the church without embarrassment and without pressure. The pastor, through preaching and teaching, needs to show people what evangelism looks like in practice, help them develop real skills for doing it, and give them the confidence that it is their own honest faith, not something formal and fancy, that is worth sharing.

Celebrating success: When we are busy with our heads down, working on one task after another, it is hard to remember to stop once in a while and look at what we have accomplished. Celebrations are more than just a good time, but they should at least be a good time—a time to enjoy a sense of accomplishment for work done. When the fruit of the work is hard to see, it is still important to celebrate the effort and dedication that went into it. Even more important, a celebration is a time to remember why we did what we did, to recommit ourselves to our overall goals, and to take the deep breath that will propel us into our next period of effort.

Starting new groups and classes: There are lots of different ways to approach any particular area of practicing our faith. Loving our neighbors, communicating with God in prayer, and offering forgiveness to those who wronged us are always current issues. A pastor, seeing the need for a particular area of growth within the family, is often the one to suggest a new approach. Any topic can be approached in many ways—through Scripture study, through topical study, through a book discussion study, through a support group, etc.—and a new way of seeing and talking about a familiar topic can bring new insights and new enthusiasm.

Encouraging people to use their gifts in new ways: When a pastor looks broadly at the idea of living out the gospel, opportunities will naturally emerge for people to participate in unfamiliar ways. This is a good thing, and the pastor can point even longtime members into new opportunities as well as engage new people in places where they may be able to connect and grow.

If you are a small-church pastor, you are probably always looking at the intersection between the commandments of Christ and the lives of the people. You have a unique perspective, knowing both the people and the gospel. This dual perspective makes it possible for you to provide the foundation and context out of which the specific activities of each individual's life of faith emerge.

THE PASTOR IS A RESOURCE FOR THE MINISTRY OF THE PEOPLE.

The ministry of the church is always the work of the people, not the job of the pastor. I have even known some churches to say on their staff list part of the bulletin, "Pastor, John Smith; Ministers, the people of the congregation." For the broad work of ministry, a pastor is an enabler and a supporter, but the pastor should never be the primary actor.

How does a pastor become an enabler? The pastor is not "in charge," making detailed plans and giving the people specific marching orders, as if the pastor were some kind of military commander and the people were the staff under orders. The work of ministry in a small church is definitely not a tightly controlled, efficiently run staff operation. Ministry is a cooperative effort of thoughtful individuals.

The pastor's job is to evoke and to support the individual ministries of the people of the church family. The pastor looks and listens for the work of the Holy Spirit in each individual's life and heart. The pastor is a helper, helping a person to listen for and to hear the Lord's particular calling for him or her. The pastor helps people respond to each of their individual callings by helping each one prepare for specific activities in response to the call and by providing encouragement along the way. The pastor also keeps a watchful eye one the people as they go forward and is there when things go badly to help get the work back on track.

How does a pastor actually do this? It may not sound like much, but a pastor asks open but directed questions, listens while a person thinks though his or her own ideas, and gently offers specific suggestions that might be helpful. These suggestions can include ways of organizing the work, other people to invite to become involved in it, places to go for resources that might be needed, contacts with others who have done similar work in the past, and sources of information about other existing policies and organizations that might impact the work. The pastor is careful not to overwhelm the individual with suggestions, but pick the few that will support and be in resonance with the ideas and approach the individual is already using.

The pastor is a cheerleader for each person's individual ministry, both to the person directly and to the wider church family. For the person, the pastor is a sounding board for ideas and also a holder of vision—reminding the person, when hip-deep in alligators, about the original goal of draining the swamp. The pastor also advertises and shares news of the work with the rest of the church family, making sure that the word shared includes the vision, scope, progress, and achievements of those involved. The pastor holds up each ministry, both to encourage the participants and to motivate onlookers in their own work, all as part of the process of building up the body of Christ.

If you are a small-church pastor, you know that encouragement can be a very delicate process. Because you know your people, you know who is enthusiastically optimistic and who sees the dark side of potential obstacles more clearly. You will know to caution one about possible problems and to encourage the other to see paths around the obstacles. Sometimes your biggest challenge will simply be keeping quiet, not offering all your best ideas so that the budding ideas from a heart growing in faith will have a chance to flower.

THE PASTOR MODELS CONNECTION AND RELATIONSHIPS.

One very important part of the pastor's work is to model Christlike relationships for the church family. Pastors show this in their encouragement of callings, but they also are visible examples in all kinds of other encounters. Pastors must be quite intentional, in all the day-to-day relationships of the church, to demonstrate what it looks like and feels like to be loving, forgiving, non-judgmental, truthful, and respectful of the dignity of every individual. The best way to teach healthy relationships is to consciously engage people in them.

A small-church pastor will have lots of opportunities to demonstrate Christlike behavior in relationships. How do you react to an off-color joke? What do you say when presented with a piece of malicious gossip? How do you react to the tale of a shady business deal or of taking advantage of a customer who didn't know any better? How do you treat children in conversation? How do you treat those who have trouble expressing themselves? Each interaction you have will be a lesson not only for the person you are talking with, but also for the other listeners and all their regular friends.

Hating the sin but loving the sinner is an easy principle to agree with, but much harder hard to actually live out. Having conversations that are clearly affirming of a person who is behaving badly, but also clearly disapproving of the wrong behavior, is not easy. I have found, for example, that a conversation with a teen caught in some form of bad behavior needs to include elements of both "You're smarter than that" and "You know you shouldn't be doing it." Most of the time, of course, you don't even need to use words. An affirmative but informed comment or gesture—for example, about a teen's smoking—typically leads to their responding, "I know it's not a good idea." If you are willing to keep on listening, you will almost always hear some kind of internal resolution to do better. I find that telling someone that they shouldn't be doing something has almost no effect at all. Supporting an attempt to change that comes from within has much more potential for success.

When pastors model this combination of truth and love, those around them pick it up. Sometimes it is enough to provide folks with some sample language to use, or even some specific ideas of things that one might say in a complicated or sensitive situation.

Of course, a pastor must model the open welcome of all people into the kingdom of God. Since all sin and fall short of the glory of God, no particular sin should lead to better or worse treatment than any other; we are all sinners together. The pastor needs to model this intentionally; for example, giving an equal welcome to each person coming into the church no matter how well dressed, well connected, or thoroughly disliked. I remind folks that it is particularly important to encourage people in need of repentance who come to church, even if what they need to repent of is something nasty they did to you personally. As a pastor, you must also lead and model this kind of forgiving welcome, especially to those who have hurt you personally. What you say and do will be noticed, and your example will circulate farther than the words of your sermon.

Pastors are also models for relationships with others in the wider community. I believe that it is important for clergy to support each other, regardless of denomination and political positions. If we are not cordial with our other brothers and sisters in Christ, however misguided we may think they are, how can we demonstrate our love for our enemies? Pastors always represent the churches they serve, and we always need to model consciously the behavior that Jesus commands of us.

If you are a small-church pastor, the behavior you model in your relationships will be one of the most widespread, and sometimes the most hidden, platforms for your ministry. When you are having a bad day, your short temper may lead to a conversation that is shared behind the scenes for years. When you act with kindness and compassion, especially when it is personally hard for you, that gift will be remembered and passed on for years. Folks are interested in behavior, particularly unexpected behavior, and your Christlike actions will speak for you.

THE PASTOR IS A GATEKEEPER.

There are many, many more worthy opportunities for service out in the world than any small church can address. The reality is that all resources are limited, particularly our resources of money and time, and we all would like to spend each dollar or each hour in several different ways at the same time.

Every week, our small church receives several phone calls from people looking for the "youth minister," the "music director," or the "business manager." The people on the other end of these phone calls generally have wonderful things to offer a church for some nominal cost. Folks have offered me various programs to revitalize out youth group, to provide wonderful retreat settings, to guide us through rewarding mission trips, and to offer us a fun time at their shows and theme parks.

Pastors typically receive several pieces of mail every day with appeals for support—either money or time or both—for completely worthy causes. There are opportunities to serve disaster victims, the homeless, those in prisons, the hungry, the mentally ill, those in recovery, victims of crimes, victims of abuse, victims of injustice, and many more who need and deserve to be helped, in this country and all over the world. How do we decide which appeals we can respond to?

The pastor of a small church is the first line of defense against the overwhelming level of need in the world. The flood of requests, when looked at as a whole, is likely to lead us to despair and inaction, because of the small impact any given church can have on the immense bulk of needs. The pastor needs to select and filter the many requests, identifying those that show promise as a match for the callings and capabilities of the congregation.

The pastor has to decide which opportunities to pass on to other individuals, which invitations to share with the congregation, and which must quietly disappear. Each pastor needs to have some policies that help determine whether an invitation to a fundraiser, an appeal for money, or a request for volunteers gets posted on the bulletin board, mentioned in the announcements, publicized with a bulletin insert, or dropped into the circular file.

When the pastor is an effective gatekeeper, opportunities that match the congregation's priorities and callings will get through, and the mass of other good causes will not. As a pastor, of course, I have trouble throwing away reasonable appeals from those in honest and desperate need, but the reality is that a small church can only do so much to alleviate the suffering of the world. For a pastor, even going through the day's mail needs to be a prayerful experience.

If you are a small-church pastor, you know how this feels. Your heart goes out to the faces you see. You ache to help the suffering captured so poignantly. You reach around in your mind for someone who would be able to take on this particular need. Then, looking at the next appeal, you struggle to compare the two. Which of those children needs help the most? You know that they all do. Which of the injustices so clearly described makes you the most angry? Again, the competition doesn't have a winner. They are all offensive. How do these needs fit into your already-stretched resources and the needs you already support?

This is where you, as a spiritual leader, need to engage your own spiritual life. You can ask advice from others, but your own prayer and discernment are your best help. Where is God leading you, and where is God leading your people? While many choices may be easy, many also will not be obvious. Your own listening to God in prayer is your best help in deciding when the gates should allow a request to pass through and when the gates should remain shut to allow the people to follow through with their present commitments.

QUESTIONS FOR REFLECTION AND DISCUSSION

1. What kinds of tasks and events in your pastor's life are predictable?
2. What kinds of surprises and crises does your pastor need to respond to?
3. How does the pastor express your church's vision and identity?
4. How does your pastor model leadership and caring relationships?
5. What kinds of support does your pastor give to the ministries of the people?

14

Pastoral Care as Facilitation

HOW DO PASTORAL CARE AND DISCIPLING HAPPEN?

IN A SMALL CHURCH, pastoral care and discipling are two processes that blend together. Situations that lead to the need for pastoral care almost always turn out to be opportunities to grow in understanding and in the practice of faith.

Pastoral care and helping people grow as disciples are both tasks that a pastor does, but they do not "belong" to the pastor alone. They are also practices that a pastor models, teaches, and passes on to the members of the congregation. All of the people of the church family, at one time or another, will have the chance to care for others and to help other grow as disciples.

Both caring and discipling happen face to face, in the direct personal contact that is part of a longstanding relationship. In those relationships, while there may be intense moments from time to time, a particular interaction is always in the context of an extended pattern of comforting, learning/teaching, and fostering spiritual growth. Over time, periods of instability and opportunity are balanced by periods of integration and practice.

In a small church, there should always be an expectation that what is received will be passed on to others. Those who came to faith through the witness of another should expect to pass on their own story. Those who loved to learn in Bible study should expect to assist and eventually teach others, using what they learned. One who was helped through a loss will be a good person to understand what the next person who suffers a loss needs most and be able to offer it gently. This pattern of receiving and passing on is a normal part of both caring ministry and discipleship within the small-church family.

The pastor has two roles in this process—doing it and teaching it. A congregation can easily get into the mindset that pastoral care and discipling are things the pastor does and the people receive. It is important for the pastor to be quite explicit about the fact that this is simply not true. Sometimes, the pastor even needs to leave space for other members of the church family to grow into these roles, while at the same time preparing them and equipping them to do this kind of ministry.

Let me give you an example of the way this can work. One Sunday, as I was greeting people at the door after the service, a woman who had lost her husband a month earlier said she was mad at herself for not having "gotten over it by now." With the crowds around, I couldn't talk to her privately, so I asked her to go, right then, to a man who had lost his wife a year earlier. Later, I saw them deep in conversation at the back of the church. The next day, this man called me to say what an honor it had been to listen and to assure her that what she was experiencing was to be expected under the circumstances. Both were blessed by each other's presence.

When caring is shared between members of the church family, the blessing flows in both directions. Both participants are blessed. Pastors can see that they have been successful when members of the church family simply step in to do what caring is needed because they are ready, willing, and able to minister to each other.

If you are a small-church pastor, you should be continually looking for ways that one congregant's experience may relate to another. One man who has just lost his job may benefit from the sympathy and help of the woman who just found work after a long search process. One who is fighting to stay clean from an addiction may appreciate the friendship of the long-recovering alcoholic. One whose father has just been diagnosed with Alzheimer's can appreciate the support of the other whose mother died last year after a long struggle with it. As pastor, you are a sort of matchmaker, helping your people find each other when there is a chance to give and receive love and care.

WHERE DO PASTORAL CARE
AND DISCIPLING HAPPEN?

In my church, and I suspect in many small churches, formal appointments for meetings between pastors and congregants mostly don't work. People don't want to take the pastor's time unless an issue has become critically important, and by then it usually has turned into an emergency with no time for a formal appointment.

My people also did not seem to be comfortable with the formality of office visits, since meeting in an office work space is not our natural element. Similarly, inviting the pastor to visit at home calls for the best china and days spent cleaning up the house.

So where do the pastor and the people come together most easily? Just about anywhere else: on the front porch, in the church kitchen, or in the parking lot. When does a meeting happen? Whenever it fits: before or after church, during coffee hour, or whenever you happen to see the pastor out in the yard, in the mall, or at social events in town. Our folk are much more comfortable "dropping by" to chat about something that would have to become a big deal if you need to schedule an office visit.

When I came to my first church, I scheduled a time when the church would be open during the week for prayer, one hour each day at dinnertime. We called this time "open sanctuary," and it resulted in an unexpected benefit. With this time slot scheduled, people knew where and when they could usually find the pastor. They could comfortably drop by for a chat about whatever big or little thing was on their minds without making a big deal of it. I tended to have a few visits during that time each week. Days when it was quiet, I had some extra time for prayer myself.

It is important for the pastor of a small church to be sensitive to when and how people make connections, and then to be available in that place. Some towns have a coffee place or a donut shop where people gather or pass through most mornings. One urban pastor I know was often found at the fast food place across the street from the church, and folks who would never pass through the church doors knew that they could find him there. One pastor may find these connections in the Scouts, another through the Little League or soccer, and another at the local gym. Points of connection like these always come out of the lifestyle and culture of the church family, and the pastor needs to join in as any other member of the family.

Does your town have a morning "hang out" place? I have found that many do, and that the conversation around and between the tables will tell you what is really going on in town. Do you as a pastor feel comfortable there? Hopefully you do. Jesus used to get a lot of flack from hanging out where the ordinary locals hung out, but he found the connection to be worth making.

PERSONAL CONNECTIONS ARE GOOD FOR EVERYONE.

There are three things I know of that will almost always make things better across a wide variety of difficulties. They will not fix the underlying causes of a problem situation, but they will work toward physical and spiritual health for the people involved. They are (1) connection with other people, (2) control over one's own life, and (3) making a contribution in the lives of others. Insofar as it is possible, a pastor's work can have a significant positive impact when it leads to improvement in any of these three areas. We will consider the way these work in turn in this and the next sections.

Connection with others happens everywhere, and it doesn't depend on a person's physical condition, however good or bad that might be. My friend and fellow pastor's mother-in-law moved to our area to live in a nursing home when she was quite elderly and completely disabled by arthritis. When she died eighteen months later, the number of friends, especially young people, who spoke at her funeral was amazing. The first teens got to know her when they visited their aunt at the same nursing home, and they found that she was such a neat person to talk with that they introduced her to their friends. From her bed with nothing but her voice and her personality, she became a light in these teens' lives.

Being confined to bed doesn't prevent connections, and being unable to leave home doesn't prevent them either. One woman I know has a regular pattern of people to chat with on the phone—some daily, some weekly, and some every once in a while. She even writes the names on the calendar so she does not lose track of contact with people she likes. She is a communicator, and when she learns of a problem or a need from someone less well-off than herself, she passes it along. Hers is a ministry of connections: her own connections with her old friends, her reaching out to others who are lonely at home, and her making connections for those others who have specific needs.

Pastoral care can facilitate connections, not just by the pastor's being connected to each person, but also by making sure that each person is connected to others. Providing the occasion for connections and encouraging them is an important ministry. This is why coffee hour and other fellowship events are caring ministries and not just superfluous social occasions. In a small church, "social" events are the settings in which we play out the dramas of our spiritual lives.

If you are a small-church pastor, you support and encourage the relationships in the congregation. You realize that social opportunities are important, especially for those who have fewer of them. You also encourage a depth of connection between people in social occasions, when it seems appropriate. One wise statesman once said, "Socializing is a device for avoiding communication." As a pastor, you have the opportunity to encourage real communication and mutual support by modeling personal truth, and not just fluff, in conversation.

MORE PERSONAL CONTROL IS ACTUALLY HEALTHY.

Having control over one's own body and one's own life also leads to better health, physically, psychologically, and spiritually. With age and with illness, a person's physical capabilities and control over his or her own body and activities deteriorate. Pastoral care needs to work against the inevitability of this loss of control.

For example, consider our dear friend Brad. Brad was almost totally paralyzed with ALS, and at one point in time several years ago, he was so depressed that he was ready to go off life support. One of the nurses in the church has been part of his care team, and she saw his interest in life grow over the years since that low point.

What kind of control can you have when you are totally paralyzed and on life support? One Monday, Brad's wife asked the nurse to cut Brad's hair. The nurse asked him if he would like to have his hair cut that day, and he said "no" with his eyes. When his wife got home from work, she wanted to know why his hair was not cut. "He didn't want me to," said the nurse. On Tuesday the answer was "no" again, but on Wednesday, he was ready for the haircut. That was when he got it.

Brad got a new dog a while back, and the dog sat by his bed, especially when there were visitors. She was a gentle older dog and fit into the family well. Brad had wanted a male dog so that he could name it after

Otis Redding, one of his favorite musicians. He ended up owning one of the only female dogs named Otis, and she doesn't seem to mind.

Often people do not realize how important personal control can be, and pastoral care defends a person's dignity and self-respect by encouraging control. Sometimes it is the person who needs to be reminded that his or her own choices matter. Sometimes it is family, friends, and caregivers who need to be reminded, by word and example, that physical control is critical to mental health. When the pastor leads on this issue, most people pick up the example quickly.

If you are a small-church pastor, you will have people in your care who are losing control: people who can't do the things they used to do. They can feel helpless, hopeless, and useless as their situations progress. You can have an immediate impact by helping find ways to regain control, even though the scope of the activities may be different. Activities that once required a car can use telephone, mail, or even email. Meetings can move from evenings to daytime. Folks can be encouraged to contribute their wisdom, expertise, and the experience of years of participation. Most important is to look for and encourage substitutes for those losses that are most important to each particular individual, so that some form of real control can replace what is lost.

DOING FOR OTHERS IS GOOD FOR THE DOER, TOO.

Encouraging people to find a way to make a contribution in the lives of others is a work of pastoral care. We do the work of the church and reach out in mission on principle, because those actions ought to be done. But doing those things for others is also good for our mental and spiritual health, and, as a result, good for our physical health as well. Pastoral care serves the people of the small church by helping them find their individual ministries and equipping them for action, because this action is good for them.

The need for a sense of meaning in life, the sense that one is making a contribution that matters, is critical to physical as well as psychological and spiritual health. In my own life, coming to faith in the first place was a result of the lack of a sense of meaning. The book entitled *When Everything You Ever Wanted Isn't Enough* seemed to describe my situation exactly. My doctor was even more blunt when he said, "You'd better find a job that you can love, or it's going to kill you." Helping people in the church find meaningful work that they can love is an important part of a pastor's care.

In many cases, what matters is not the specific work we do, but the meaning that we find in it. For example, our deacons have always been a group of people with active gifts for caring, and they have served those in need inside and outside the church family. They work hard and conscientiously, and sometimes they can get burned out just doing the work. Since they are usually more comfortable doing for others than talking about why they do what they do, we recently went through an exercise of sharing faith stories.

What do you think we learned from listening to each other? We found that there was a common theme in the experiences of all of our deacons. Their common experience of life, either before they came to believe or when they were away from the church, was of emptiness, of a longing that nothing else would satisfy. It was only by being part of God's family and doing God's work there that they found a sense of completeness, a sense of doing what they were created to do.

Working as a leader in a small church includes helping people find those places where their gifts and talents, skills and interests, meet the needs of the world. Whether you are a pastor, a leader, or simply a participant in a small church, part of your role is to help the people around you find, explore, and grow into their own particular ministries. In the context of our long-term relationships, we all help each other to find and share the work that gives our lives meaning.

FOR PASTORS, LISTENING COMES FIRST.

Pastoral care is always, always, always, and especially in the small church, about listening. Listening is not easy when we are sure that we have in mind the right solution to whatever problem we are facing at the moment. Listening is even harder when we hear anguish and have not the slightest idea of what to do about it. But listen we must, regardless of how uncomfortable inside we may be at the time.

What we, as pastors and leaders in a small-church family, bring to a person who is struggling with a difficulty is our simple presence. We are there with the other and for the other, whether we agree or not, whether we are friends or not, and whether we can do anything about the situation or not. We are there as witnesses to who this person is, what this person cares about, and what is happening in this person's life. We bring the presence of God through God's family into that place, and just by being there we are, in fact, doing something real.

In seminary, they called this just being there a "non-anxious presence," and I think this is a good way of describing it. We must leave all our own anxieties outside the door—our busyness, our own worries, our inadequacies, and our concerns about the other person's situation. We are simply ourselves, ready to be there, wherever the concerns may lead and for whatever kind of support may be needed.

When you are listening, you can never tell what the other person might need, no matter how well you think you know that person. Some might need to express their secret fears, knowing that you are a safe listener and will not contradict or be upset. Some may need to express their anger or frustration, knowing that you won't make them feel silly if they let down their guard. Some may need to laugh, even in the face of death, at the irony and foolishness of the human condition. A supportive and listening presence follows sympathetically wherever the other may lead.

Of course, our listening is not all agreement. When a person says something we believe to be wrong, we can disagree gently without making an argument about it. Simply saying, "I don't see it that way," or "You know we have different ideas about that," should be enough to mark the difference without interrupting the real message of personal support. When the person says something that shows understanding and insight—seeing the hand of God at work in the situation—we are in a place to affirm it, highlight it, and hold it in memory.

A friend of mine in seminary used to say, "I don't know what I think until I hear myself say it." Much of what we hear may be tentative, expressing conflicting feelings and trying out alternatives to find what feels right. Our role as listener is to affirm and accentuate the healthy: those thoughts and feelings that are God-inspired and that will ultimately lead toward health.

In pastoral care, whether coming from the pastor or from any other member of the church family, telling a person in crisis what to do or how to think simply does not work. What we need to do is listen and wait for the person's own insight to come out, and then appreciate what we have heard. This way, individuals can find their own course, can own it, and are in the place to be able to make things happen for themselves.

I will never forget one heart patient I met in the hospital, a truck driver who grew up in the city. He needed to laugh, and we were in stitches over the summer he spent on a farm in Iowa driving a combine. At one point he said, "You know, I've been promising *him* (pointing upward) that I was going to change my life. What I should have been doing is promising *me*." In his own way and in his own time, he had come to a serious theological insight about free will and personal responsibility. By the time he was ready to leave the hospital, his plans for the future reflected his determination to live out of this new mindset.

If you are the pastor of a small church, you have the honor and joy of witnessing this kind of transformation. This is not work that you do, but that the person in your care does with God's help. Your job is to make the space where such insights can emerge and to affirm them when they do. The privilege of seeing God at work firsthand is so great that you do not want to mess it up by inserting your own ego into the conversation.

QUESTIONS FOR REFLECTION AND DISCUSSION

1. How hard or easy is it for the people of your church to go to the pastor for help?

2. What do you hope to find when you go to your pastor?

3. How does your pastor encourage you? How do you encourage others?

4. Is your pastor a good listener? Are you a good listener? How can you be better?

15

Discipling through Personal Relationships

SPIRITUAL DIRECTION IS A DAILY PRACTICE.

I BELIEVE THAT SPIRITUAL direction, like certain other famous phrases, is a contradiction in terms. No one can direct the spiritual growth of another, and no one can direct the work of the Holy Spirit in any way. The work of a spiritual director, as I understand it, is much more like the role of a midwife or birthing coach—to stand by, to encourage, to explain what is happening, and to help the person doing the real work to thrive through the process.

I once worked with a spiritual director to do a guided retreat through the *Spiritual Exercises* of Ignatius of Loyola. The director made it quite clear: "I don't run this retreat; the Holy Spirit does." In all our work to help people grow in their spiritual lives, this one principle is the most important to remember. Spiritual growth is a work between God and the individual soul; the rest of us are just supporting actors in the drama.

Our spiritual life is grounded in our relationship with God, and that relationship is often compared to a marriage. As in a marriage, the relationship is a living, ongoing thing, not a contract to be signed and then filed away. Like a marriage, a relationship with God requires ongoing communication based in love and trust. As with a marriage, our relationship with God changes over time, growing stronger and closer over the years, but also going through periods that are more and less satisfying.

What does "spiritual direction" do for our relationship with God? A spiritual director can act like a marriage counselor in our spiritual life, helping us over the bleak spots and keeping us on track to grow in faith and love.

Small-church people may not think consciously about spiritual direction, but they do turn to their pastors quietly for help with their spiritual lives. The symptom they are most likely to notice and mention is "some kind of trouble praying," or that it has been "hard to pray" lately. This kind of opening is a wonderful opportunity to help a person grow in his or her life of faith. The pastor has the great honor of a front row seat to see the work of God in a human life and soul. With prayerful listening, the pastor tries to discern the work of the Spirit—the issue at the root of the struggle, the theological principles that are being engaged, and the guidance in Scripture that is relevant to the situation.

Often, the person, if he or she is among the longtime faithful of a small church, already has heard and known most of the principles involved. Usually all that is needed from the pastor is gentle questioning: How does this thing that Jesus said apply? How is this like what Paul was talking about? How did Jeremiah or Job respond when he felt this way?

Those who have been part of the church for years and are committed to being guided by Scripture often only need to be reminded of the relevant passages to engage them prayerfully. Newcomers and those who are still learning their way around the Scriptures will need more time and context to digest the guidance they find there. Wherever a person is on their path of growing in the knowledge and love of God, even when, as sometimes happens, they are farther along that path than the pastor, a fresh perspective on relevant Scripture can be helpful.

If you are the pastor of a small church, you will find yourself encouraging growth in faith when your folks express a need or discomfort, while they may not even consciously experience this need as a spiritual issue. You may never have thought of yourself as a spiritual director, but you are engaging a person who needs guidance in his or her spiritual life. You reach into your own experience of God and the reality that your faith has for you to find your response. When your teaching comes in response to a felt need, the word you share speaks directly into the life situation of the growing disciple.

FAITH GROWS IN AND THROUGH CRISIS.

The one time that people seem to recognize that they need the church and their faith, other than to give Christian values to their children, is when something goes wrong. In times of crisis—a serious illness, the death of a loved one, unfaithfulness in marriage, loss of a job—it suddenly becomes clear that we need more strength than life as usual requires.

Illness and death and loss are part of the normal human condition, as much as we may have come to believe that they are optional in the modern world. Shock, anger, and complaints against God are only human, and we see them often in our scriptural tradition. Confidence in the future life while we are grieving in the present is part of our faith, as we enjoy the mix of experiences in this life while we are waiting for the joy of eternal life.

The pastor's role is to walk with each person through crisis at the level of involvement that each person needs. The pastor's role is to bring reminders of God's eternal love and care into the multitude of considerations and action items that a crisis entails. The pastor's job is to listen and encourage as each person tries to make sense of what God is doing through this painful time.

For pastors, there can be some comfort in accepting what we do not know and in trusting that things are in God's hands. One of my favorite stories involves a man who decides to enjoy all of the sins of this life, and then have a deathbed conversion to get into heaven. His life is full of pleasures, and at the end he calls for a priest, confesses his sins, and dies. Does he get into heaven after all? We really don't know, and nor does the priest. If the man's confession was sincere, if he looks back on his life as the waste it was and repents, then the answer is "yes." If his confession is the planned formula, with secret satisfaction that he got away with it all, then the answer is "no." That confession, if not true and sincere, can not trick God into letting him into a reward. Only God, who sees into the heart, knows. We as pastors can only trust God to be just as well as merciful.

Faith and trust in God are almost always challenged during a crisis. Faith is part of the strength that helps us put one foot in front of the other during the crisis, and faith is a critical part of rebuilding life afterward. There are times when life can deal a person a really nasty hand, and the pastor does no service by pretending that the situation is any better than it is. The pastor's place is with the person who is suffering, walking with him or her right through the valley of the shadow of death, acting as a visible token of God's presence, which is also there.

Part of the pastor's role is also to refer people to other sources of help: grief counselors, support groups, and other kinds of psychological services. In my experience, the people of small churches are less likely than usual to take advantage of these resources and may need extra encouragement. Small-church people more often look for comfort and support within the church family, and sometimes the pastor will see the opportunity to bring together those who can support each other.

For a small-church pastor, times of crisis can be your greatest challenge and your greatest opportunity to make a difference. Your people are vulnerable and thrown out of their normal routine and complacency. They are often overwhelmed as well as hurting, and they know vaguely that the church is the place to go for help. In crisis, your kindness and compassion and love can be sought without embarrassment and accepted without pride. You have your best opportunity to act for Christ and witness to the presence of God through the time of trial.

ALWAYS BE READY FOR SPONTANEOUS TEACHING MOMENTS.

Even when there is not a current crisis, pastors are somehow "experts" on what God thinks and expects. People come to the pastor of a small church with the most incredible range of questions and situations. Ann Landers used to say that there was no way she could be creative enough to make up some of the letters people sent her. Small-church people may look like ordinary, everyday folks, but the drama behind their lives is often worthy of Shakespeare.

Sin, of course, is a big part of most drama. In my experience, sex, rather than money, seems to be the most popular topic. Jealousy and marital infidelity in their many forms emerge in the lives of all kinds of people, not just the rich and famous. Domestic violence is unexpectedly real, as I found out talking with one dignified widow who said, "The day that man died was the best day of my life, because finally I knew I was safe." Folks struggle with all sorts of temptation, and sometimes they come to the pastor for some strong arguments to help them do what they already know is the right thing.

A small-church pastor needs always to be "prayed up" to be ready for anything. I think the least expected question for me came from a teen-aged boy. A girl who was "just a friend" of his was having trouble with her best friend and had come to him for help. The best friend had just decided to become a lesbian and wanted to have sex. How should he tell this girl to respond? Since I am convinced that sex outside of a marriage covenant is not appropriate, I knew what I meant to say. But how to express it in this context was not as easy, and I needed a lot of help from the Holy Spirit. He was glad to have more than just his uneasy feeling to go on to tell her it was not a good idea.

Teaching moments happen often as we bump along in our lives together. At one point, I was listening to the long story of who did what to whom in a complicated family of mother and daughters, all with strong characters. In the end, I had no need to give my opinion. The mother, listening to herself, said, "I know I should forgive, but I just can't . . . yet."

One young man visited me when he needed to move back in with his parents for a while. When I asked what was going on, he reacted to me as if I were his mother criticizing his choice of friends, saying defensively, "I know I shouldn't hang out with those guys." You could see his shock when I said, "Well, that's really up to you." The light dawned as he realized that he really was an adult in control of his own choices, and that, even though he was living with his parents again, he didn't have to rebel automatically any more.

The beauty of these moments is that they provide an opening to bring the gospel into the place where the rubber meets the road in the ordinary incidents of everyday life. When an issue comes up, you have the person's attention. He or she is already motivated to figure out what to do, open to the pastor's help. Even better, if this person has been part of the church family for any length of time, the answer to the problem has already crossed the airwaves at least once. The pastor can use a very light touch, not to tell them what to do, but to make the connection between what they are facing and the teaching they have already known and accepted.

You can be sure that you can relate to the people of the small church if you know one or both of the people in the following story, which came from the legends of the Internet:

> Mildred, the church gossip and self-appointed monitor of the church's morals, kept sticking her nose into other people's business. Several members did not approve of her nasty habit, but feared her enough to maintain their silence.
>
> She made a mistake, however, when she accused Henry, a new member, of being an alcoholic after she saw his old pickup parked in front of the town's only bar one afternoon.

She emphatically told Henry, and several others, that everyone seeing it there knew what he was doing and what his problem was. Henry, a man of few words, stared at her for a moment and just turned and walked away. He didn't explain, defend, or deny. He said nothing.

Later that evening, Henry quietly parked his pickup in front of Mildred's house, walked home, and left it there all night. You gotta love Henry.

Sin, self-righteousness, and mischievous fun are all intertwined in small-church life. You can be sure you will enjoy pastoral care in the small church if you just can't wait to be part of the many teaching moments that will unfold as the repercussions of this incident echo around the church family.

WATCH FOR CHANCES TO AFFIRM THE POSITIVE.

Small churches have an especially bad reputation, particularly among new, young, enthusiastic pastors, for being resistant to change. The pastor comes, full of the latest insights and glorious plans, to find unexplained resistance and an unwillingness to move away from old ways. It just does not make sense, and, within a few years, the discouraged and disgusted new pastor moves on.

From the old-timers' point of view, something quite different is happening. New pastors have come and gone over the years, each with some new approach or program that they were excited about. Just as their new idea was getting started, someone would stop by from the outside, see the exciting potential, and offer the pastor a new job somewhere else. The church would be left with a half-finished project, with no one to advocate for it or lead it. Grafting new ideas into the church from the outside can be a risky business.

A more effective approach to change in the small church is to let a new thing grow out of the things the church family already does well, or out of the gifts, interests, and callings of individuals in the congregation. This way, regardless of how long the pastor is able to stay—and a personal crisis can hit any pastor at any age—the new ministry belongs to the church and not to the pastor.

This approach to leadership requires a very light touch on the part of the pastor. Yes, the pastor can provide a buffet of possibilities from the best current wisdom, but what a particular church will be able to do depends on which activities particular individuals are willing to put on their own plates. Piling plates high with options folks do not understand or want just leads to spiritual indigestion and loss of appetite. In most cases, it is more effective to let people get a little hungry and then show them sample menus, rather than to prepare a whole feast for them in advance.

What does it take to help the people of a small church lead themselves into the future? It takes a lot of listening, a well-chosen array of suggestions held in reserve, and a lot of affirmation of the positive in what we see and hear.

What kinds of positive thoughts can we affirm and encourage as we listen? One is a sense of calling, a hunger to respond to some aspect of the gospel message. Another is a sense of giftedness, a sense that we have something worth sharing that could be used in service. Another is a cry of the heart, an empathy for those suffering with specific needs that touch a particular chord. Another is the realization that what worked in reaching out to one person by chance might also work for others if we got ourselves organized.

Good ideas can come from anywhere: from the Bible to the evening news, as well as from rumors about what other churches are doing or from memories of what worked years ago. The pastor gets to listen a lot, ask questions, and offer to find information and resources that might be helpful. In a small church, every project or idea needs to have one or more originators and owners. The pastor should never be the primary advocate for an idea, although the pastor should pay attention and be available with whatever kind of support and guidance is needed.

A pastor should be the cheerleader and visionary for the church family, the holder of the big picture of the direction of the whole community. The pastor should always be able to explain, giving appropriate credit, what the church is doing and why. The pastor holds the vision of the way each particular effort fits into the work of the kingdom of God in our midst. The pastor is the one to reflect back to each participant the value and significance of his or her work as part of the work of Christ on earth.

Pastors affirm the positive in individual lives by witnessing to the work of the Holy Spirit. Pastors are in a unique position to see each individual's growth in faith and to help that person see from the outside what he or she may not even have noticed was happening on the inside. Pastors are the right people to notice and make others aware of individual progress and achievement, celebrating what each person in their midst is capable of doing.

Affirming the positive is a continuing process for a small-church pastor, and, to do it well, you need to love watching people grow. Mentoring, coaching, and discipling all entail personal involvement and empathy with the people. While watching, you are helping your people think theologically about everyday events and relationships so that they see the implications and impacts of their own lives. In return, you as pastor get an unparalleled opportunity to watch the work of the kingdom of God in action.

QUESTIONS FOR REFLECTION AND DISCUSSION

1. What formal discipleship programs does your church offer?
2. How are you growing in your faith? How is the church helping you grow?
3. What incidents—events or conversations—have helped you grow in faith?
4. How can you emphasize and encourage the positive, notice and appreciate the good things you see?

16

Living as an Example

Life in a Fishbowl

EVERYBODY KNOWS EVERYBODY ELSE'S BUSINESS.

Life in a small church is like life in a small town, only more so. All interactions between people, which include every meeting that the pastor has with anyone else, are likely to become public knowledge. People will know how you spend your time and even how you get along with members of your own family. If you are thinking of being the pastor of a small church and this idea bothers you, you need to think again.

Members of a small church in a rural area or urban neighborhood tend to have many more points of contact than simply being in the same place at the same time on Sunday morning. They typically buy their food at one of a small number of grocery stores, take their nights out at one of a few local restaurants, and go to the local hospital when they get sick. Often, they work in these places as well, or have friends who do. They see each other at the closest mall. They know each other's habits, hangouts, and preferences.

They also know and recognize each other's cars, and this gives each person a window into each other person's activities. If a car is parked in front of a particular tavern or spends the night in someone else's driveway, this is public information. Even a person's normal evening walk, and the exceptions to it, are closely understood.

There was a wonderful illustration of this effect on a television comedy about the life of a small-town minister. The pastor's family started receiving "helpful" information about their husband and father—how he was seen having lunch with a married woman, how he was seen hugging her, and finally how he was seen checking into a local motel with her. "Everybody" knew where the pastor was seen and in what company, and "everybody" came to their own conclusions about what it must mean.

In this particular story, all became clear when the woman appeared at the pastor's house, followed shortly by her abusive and threatening husband. It became clear to the pastor's family, but only when the woman allowed her story to be shared with them, the kind of help and support the pastor had been providing. There was a beautiful moment at the end when the pastor hugged the "other woman" and his family joined in.

I sympathize with this fictional pastor because my life has also been an open book. Which car was parked in front of my office and how long it was parked there are available for all to see. I once received a call from the mother of a troubled teen, wanting to know exactly what I was talking about with her daughter, while the daughter was sitting in my office. I have had a father, checking on his son, park around the corner and watch for the son's car to appear at the church. Many, many times I have been asked how so-and-so is doing because their car was seen parked out front.

In a small church, you can't keep secrets, and you can never tell who shares information with whom. This is simply the way it is. This should act as a deterrent for some kinds of bad behavior, but, amazingly, those who should know better seem to forget their visibility exactly when they are about to succumb to temptation. And, because we in a small church are together for a lifetime, the consequences of sin really are passed from one generation to the next.

THE APPEARANCE OF INNOCENCE IS REQUIRED.

The television minister I mentioned fell into a trap that is waiting for every pastor in a small church. He violated one of my father's favorite dictums: "Innocence is never enough; the appearance of innocence is also required." Regardless of whether you are actually guilty of any impropriety as a pastor, it is absolutely vital that you also scrupulously avoid any appearance of impropriety. It is not enough to be innocent; you have to not look guilty, either. Please note: Being innocent is still of primary importance; the point here is that the appearance matters as well.

How do pastors protect themselves from misunderstanding while protecting the confidentiality of their conversations? They hold meetings in places where they can be seen and not heard. The very first thing pastors should do when they arrive at a new office, even before carrying in their boxes of books, is to make sure that there is a window in the door. My own study was in the front room of the manse, and I made sure that whatever was going on in my study was in full view of anyone walking by on the porch, which doubled as the handicapped entrance to the church. Sometimes, meetings in public places such as restaurants or coffee shops work well. Those visiting the pastor should be able to tell that others may be passing by at any moment, just so that there is a common sense of the public visibility of any encounter.

In a small church, since fewer people are available to provide financial controls and no money is available for accounting professionals, pastors also need to make sure that money is handled safely. In my experience, the financial dangers in a small church do not come from those who intend to be thieves. Professional thieves are looking for richer targets. The danger in a small church comes from the well-meaning person, often a longtime servant of the church, who borrows a bit with the honest intent of returning the money before it is missed. This kind of person, who is the last person you would expect to steal, uses someone else's money with the best of intentions for the best of purposes. Then, one thing or another goes badly, and they are stuck in a pattern of petty crime.

The pastor in a small church needs to assume the best, but ensure against the worst of alternatives. Simple financial controls—like counting with two people when there is more than a certain amount of cash, having a second person check the bank statements, and having an independent review of the treasurer's books from time to time—should be sufficient for most situations. The nice thing about building controls into the process is that temptation can be prevented and the appearance of innocence maintained at the same time.

Processes put into place to assure the appearance of innocence may feel like a hassle, but they can save you from really bad surprises if you are a small-church pastor. You may find folks objecting to additional procedures and controls, and, if you are lucky, it will turn out that you never needed them. However, your processes that maintain the appearance of innocence also encourage innocence in fact. Although processes in a small church are largely informal, once you convince your folks that some routines are needed, they can easily become "the way we do things" with practice and repetition.

A PASTOR MUST BE SEEN TO WORK HARD.

Is it hard work to be the pastor of a small church? Interestingly, this is an area where pastors and many congregants have a difference of opinion.

A member of a congregation does not see their pastor working very often. There is the hour of worship on Sunday morning, the hospital visit last year (but that was only twenty minutes), a committee meeting or two, and a conversation when there was a problem (although that was just stopping by). Maybe it would seem to amount to about eight hours or so a week, total for everybody.

From a pastor's point of view, full-time work takes fifty or more hours each week. Sunday morning takes planning, creating the order of worship, researching and writing a sermon, coordinating with other participants in the service, arranging for music, collecting things to be shared with different people, and checking the sanctuary to make sure everything is in place. If the pastor is also teaching a class, preparation and teaching time are also needed. Coffee hour is a time for caring, not for sitting back to relax with a cup of coffee. The point is that a lot more is going on behind the scenes than the one hour that everyone sees during the worship service. In each area of activity, from worship to visiting to committee meetings, at least twice if not more time is required in preparation and follow-up than is actually visible.

Picture the pastor who has started early, for the second or third time this week, to get a good start on the sermon, but has been derailed by a stream of interruptions and phone calls (some quite important). When a hardworking deacon stops by on lunch hour and the pastor is still not dressed or shaved and ready for the day, the deacon can't help but think that the pastor has spent another lazy morning sleeping in.

My personal weakness is the afternoon nap. I start early and I work into the evening, so I try to take a break in the middle. Whether I rest right at lunchtime or wait until mid-afternoon, I seem to pick the moment that the parcel delivery needs a signature, the copier repair person arrives, or a person with a question or crisis happens to drop by. And, of course, the phone chooses that time to ring. A lot.

I do not have a solution to the potential problem of looking like you do not work very hard. It helps to give the church board regular status reports to show the way pastoral time is being spent. At least then, when questions arise, the leaders know what you have been doing and have input to the way you spend your time. Over time, the record of activity reports also remind you of what activities you actually accomplished during your many hours of effort. Talking over choices of use of time with your board also helps. The board can then support decisions to put time into curriculum as opposed to visiting, or the other way around, and the choices do not appear to be strictly personal.

TO MANSE OR NOT TO MANSE?

The great advantage for a small church with a manse or parsonage is that the cash amount needed to support a pastor is lower. Even if the pastor chooses not to live in the manse, renting the manse can at least partially offset the cost of the pastor's housing.

From the pastor's point of view, there is at least one serious financial disadvantage to living in a manse: The pastor does not build equity in real estate and does not have the opportunity to benefit from its increasing value. The various alternative arrangements, for example equity sharing, are often beyond the abilities of a small church.

The other reason a pastor may prefer not to live in a manse is to preserve a sense of personal privacy and separation between home and family and the church. In a small church, where everybody knows everybody else's business anyway, this sense of privacy and separation is strictly illusory.

I lived in a manse for more than five years, and I found it to be a good experience. It is the shortest commute I have ever had, since the house was about twelve feet from the church. My front door opened onto the church handicapped entrance ramp. Folks looking for help did come to my door from time to time. The church and manse shared a well, so I knew when water ran in the church by the sound of the pump in my basement.

Good boundaries with neighbors and church members are absolutely necessary to have a good experience living in a manse. After all, the pastor is using property that belongs to all the people, and they feel a sense of ownership for it. The worst example of lack of boundaries I remember was the pastor who found out that others had keys to the manse when she was informed that she should not be leaving dirty dishes in the kitchen sink.

In a similar way, I have known congregations who were surprised, when the pastor moved out after fifteen or eighteen or twenty years of raising a family, to find that the manse needed refurbishing and repainting. Good boundaries include an understanding of who will take care of what kinds of maintenance, and who will take care of the costs of that maintenance.

I found the people of the church I served to be very careful to respect my personal space and privacy. My office was on the first floor of the manse, and from time to time we hosted a Bible study, committee meetings, or a social event in the living room. Upstairs was strictly family territory. The fact that I am domestically challenged was well known in the congregation, so expectations of my housekeeping skills were not all that high.

Offering personal hospitality can be very important in a small church. Some of my pastor colleagues have held dinner parties for members of their congregations, and this is part of their own personal style of ministry. In a small church, it is possible to offer hospitality to the whole congregation without creating an in-group or causing some to feel left out.

However, the ability to offer hospitality also depends on good boundaries. One seminarian friend said that, in her church's culture, folks would move into the manse kitchen after church and not leave until late in the evening. The danger of welcome being taken advantage of can make it hard for pastors in some small-church cultures to offer hospitality at all.

Coming from a culture of the more reserved Northeast, the people of my church seem to have a natural respect and consideration for each other and for their pastor, which I work hard to emulate. They intend, even if they do not succeed all the time, to respect each other's feelings and space. Nowhere did I see this more clearly than in my next-door neighbor at the manse.

My neighbor's front windows looked out on the front of the church, and most evenings she was at the window, busy with her quilting. She was the one who kept an eye on things while we were away and checked out any strangers who appeared in places they are not expected to be. She has an incredible sense of tact in what she chooses to notice, both in what she observes to protect the church and our family as neighbors, and in what she chooses to ignore. I wish that every small-church pastor could have neighbors with just the right blend of caring interest and discretion.

When my neighbor had a suggestion, she made it gently and kindly. Some suggestions I followed and some I did not, and she seemed to be able to live with both. Her main concern with this book is that it has too much gossip in it. I respect her concern, but I believe that, in order to encourage each other and build up the body of Christ, we need to learn from the specifics of each other's experience.

If you become the pastor of a small church, you will have to decide for yourself how to live in close relationships. Choosing to live in a manse, which is the property of the church, can be a great help economically, but comes with the need to establish the boundaries around your own home life. I was happy with my experience, but then I was blessed by the sensitivity of the folks around me. You will need to take the culture and customs of your people into account when you make your own choices.

QUESTIONS FOR REFLECTION AND DISCUSSION

1. How does it feel for a pastor to live in a "fishbowl"?
2. How is the author's experience of visibility different from yours? How is it similar?
3. How do you feel about the importance of appearances?
4. What boundaries does your church keep to protect the pastor's private life?
5. How hard do you think your pastor works? What work is going on that you don't see?

17

Coping in a Church that Can't Afford Its Pastor

THEY WISH THEY COULD PAY MORE.

THE PEOPLE IN SMALL churches wish they were able to pay their pastor fairly. Unfortunately, most of the time, the reality is that they simply do not have enough money to do it. Our church had been struggling to pay its pastor for most of its two-hundred-year history. Our first pastor, Rev. Baldwin, faced this problem in the early 1800s:

> The congregation at that time was small and feeble, unable to support a minister properly and hence he purchased a farm, on which he lived until his death.[1]

His successor, forty years later, fared a little better:

> Receipts in the Trustee book indicate laxity in paying the first pastor. He appears to have had only one payment in two or three years sometimes of his usual salary of $300 to $350. Mr. Prime received $520 and was paid promptly.[2]

Our denomination has set minimum standard amounts that a church should pay its pastor, and this church has only rarely been able to afford these minimums. Some correspondence from the denomination's Committee on Ministerial Relations in 1947 shows the kinds of feelings on both sides of the issue:

---

1. Rev. S. W. Mills, *The Scotchtown Memorial; or The Centennial of the Scotchtown Presbyterian Church* 1796–1896, quoted in Risley, *Third Century and Counting*, 27.

2. Charles. A. Comfort, *A Sketch of Scotchtown prepared for the One Hundred and Forty Fifth Anniversary, Old Home Day*, presented on August 31, 1943, quoted in Risley, *Third Century and Counting*, 60.

> As chairman of this committee, I know that some churches are paying less than a living wage and others are paying salaries that are unworthy of their resources or of the services rendered. . . . We call upon you to deal realistically and sympathetically with the question of your pastor's salary. . . . Your minister depends entirely upon the spirit of understanding of his officers and congregation. His well being and that of his family is [sic] closely identified with the success of the onward moving program of the church. Will you make it your personal concern that your minister may be free from worry and care and so give his best serve to the building of the Kingdom in our day?[3]

When the church leaders met, they all agreed that "the pastor is supposed to be the spiritual leader of the community and that we were not paying the price of leadership." However, the letter back to the committee from the church reflects the reality of the situation:

> The increased salary of course must come from the treasury. The treasurer reported that the present salary is as much as the treasury can pay.[4]

Of course, the church does whatever it can to encourage contributions and to raise money by other means when the contributions are not enough.

> Dr. Alexander Kerr was installed in March, 1924. Our church paid Dr. Kerr $900, gave him free use of the Manse and one month's vacation. From this period on, until 1953, the Ladies Aid Society prepared many, many suppers, contributing the proceeds to the salary of the ministers.[5]

But there is always a tension between spending money for the other missions of the church and allocating the money to pay the pastor. For example,

> It is interesting to note that the reports of the different societies of the church at the annual meeting of 1933, indicated that finances were in good condition except that "we are somewhat in arrears

3. Letter to the Clerk of Session of the Scotchtown Presbyterian Church dated Jan. 30, 1947, quoted in Risley, *Third Century and Counting*, 59.

4. Reply from the Clerk of Session of the Scotchtown Presbyterian Church dated March 16, 1947, quoted in Risley, *Third Century and Counting*, 59.

5. Mabel Mills, 1797–1972 *Yesterday Today and Forever; Scotchtown Presbyterian Church*, quoted in Risley, *Third Century and Counting*, 60.

with our Pastor's salary." We find in the reports of Session for many years, a constant payment of our allotments to various causes of Presbytery or the General Assembly while we struggled without success to raise the approved minimum wage for our ministers.[6]

In a small church, there is not enough money to go around, and there is strong competition for the use of that money. The people of the church have to make hard choices about how much of their income they can give to the church, how much time they can give to other fundraising activities, and how the money will be split among pastoral, building, and mission expenses. Even with their best efforts, money to pay the pastor often comes up short.

PASTORS NEED TO LIVE AT THE ECONOMIC LEVEL OF THE PEOPLE.

Some years ago, I was sitting at breakfast on retreat with a pastor who had a history of founding new churches. One church he had led had spun off three daughter churches during his time there. Since he was probably the first person any of us around the table had met who had succeeded in starting a new church, the natural question was, "What does it take to start a new church?" His answer was immediate. He said, "Ten families, if all of them tithe."

When you think about it, ten families ought to be enough to start out. For ten families, you can eliminate building costs by worshiping in a home or borrowed space. Ten families, if each contributes 10 percent of their own income, should be able to cover a salary for their pastor that would allow the pastor's family to live at the same economic level as the other families in the church.

How realistic is this approach? In one sense, it seems reasonable that servants of Christ should not expect to live more comfortably than their people, especially when their salary comes directly from the household budgets of the people.

In another sense, based on the congregation's culture, pastors can be expected to live differently from their people, sometimes in ways that are more costly. In many churches, pastors are expected to have more education and to provide more expensive education to their own children than

6. Mabel Mills, 1797–1972 *Yesterday Today and Forever; Scotchtown Presbyterian Church*, quoted in Risley, *Third Century and Counting*, 60.

most folks in the church. In other cultures, the pastor is an icon for the whole congregation, and the clothes, car, and visible lifestyle of the pastor represent the best of what the people would like for themselves.

The real question, the one that needs to be considered by anyone thinking of pastoring a small church, is, "How important is the money to you, personally?" Pastors of small churches will never live in the kind of houses, drive the kinds of cars, or take the kinds of vacations that their classmates who went into medicine or business do. They will never be members of the country club or enjoy the kinds of entertainment that many of the pastors of affluent larger churches do. If you are considering ministry, particularly ministry in a small-church setting, you need to come to terms with the real financial constraints that living within the same means as your people will bring.

USE TIMES OF LIFE THAT REQUIRE LESS INCOME.

I am a pastoral "retread," a midlife career changer who came to ministry after a long career in the computer business. I consider it a great honor to be able to serve Jesus Christ instead of my former bosses in the financial services industry. My experience in business even seems to help in ministry sometimes, although rarely in the ways I would have expected. Because I came to ministry late in life, I have fewer years to devote to serving a congregation than those who make ministry their lifelong calling. On the other hand, this life pattern does have a few advantages.

Because I spent part of my working life in jobs that paid relatively well, I was able to do things that mattered to me, like save for my children's education and save for retirement. The high-expense phases of life—the children's braces, clothes, lessons of all kinds, equipment, summer camps, the dreaded college tuition, etc.—are all behind me. Our family needs are pretty basic—food, clothes, rent, transportation, and occasional treats—for two adults who never did develop expensive taste. This gives a level of freedom that makes it possible to work where the need is, not where the money is.

The key for me, and for others who come to ministry later in life, is that this is finally a chance to do a job I love, one that has benefit for others, and one that serves God as best I can understand what that means. For me, pastoral ministry is an honor and a privilege, a feeling only heightened by comparing this life with the things I used to have to do for a living.

One way to look at ministry in a small church is as part of a life pattern that includes periods of other kinds of work. Times of life when expenses and needs for income are relatively low are good times to serve small churches. Whether it is early career (fresh out of school and looking for experience), mid-career (looking for a break from a high-pressure environment), or late career (time to use gifts that have been on the shelf), there are times when a pastor can make the conscious choice to trade cash money for the opportunity to serve in a small church.

LOOK FOR ALTERNATIVE WAYS TO MAKE MONEY.

The Apostle Paul was the church's first bivocational pastor, although his choice occupation of making tents is no longer in demand in today's society. Viable alternative sources of income these days include practically anything someone will pay you to do that leaves you free on Sunday mornings. In my neighborhood, pastors of small churches were teachers, accountants, therapists, engineers, school bus drivers, guidance counselors, and sometimes they even did a spot of work in construction.

How would you choose what kind of work to do in addition to being a pastor? Sometimes, you can continue to use caring gifts in jobs like teaching and counseling. If you are one who needs a regular change of pace, business or contracting can be helpful for balance. If you want a job that doesn't take your mind away from the pastoral role, driving a school bus or acting as an aide in schools may take the right level of mental and emotional engagement.

What is the minimum amount of time a church needs from a part-time pastor? A minimum need would include leading worship and preaching on Sunday morning, serving communion during those services when it is offered, performing weddings and funerals as needed, chairing the monthly meeting of church leaders, and being available in times of crisis. For a small community this level of coverage could be provided in a one-quarter time position, approximately ten to twelve hours per week, or three "units" of three to four hours each.

It is possible to combine pastoral work with an otherwise full life, but it is not easy. During introductions at a class at CUME (Gordon-Conwell Theological Seminary's Center for Urban Ministerial Education), one man's life included working a full-time job, raising a family, pastoring a church, and finishing his seminary degree on the "nine-year plan." He was a gifted pastor and man of God. The path he was on took a lot of work, and I believe that in each part of his life he was doing God's work with those around him.

TRADE TIME TO PURSUE OTHER INTERESTS.

A part-time pastorate is a natural place for those who have other interests that they would like to have time to follow. The key is to look at the extra time as an asset to be spent where you care most. One rabbi in our area uses his time off to be the primary caregiver for his grandson. A pastor who is the mother of two young children has a position that is slightly more than half time in order to have time for her family commitments.

Pastors may also have personal advocacy positions that they would like to advance by investing their time. One priest I know spends half of his time working with the deaf. The senior pastor of one very large church in New York City also served in the U.S. Congress for many years. One pastor near Boston was paid for about half time, but worked easily three times that when you include her advocacy for social justice issues. In each case, the base of pastoral ministry is the foundation from which personal and political advocacy grows.

Pastors are also notorious book and education addicts, and a part-time pastorate can provide some of the extra time to use for learning. I love taking courses, not only because I learn something about the subject matter, but also because I enjoy the perspectives of the teachers and my fellow students. The amount of information and the range of educational opportunities currently available are staggering, and some material is bound to be entertaining for every interest area.

Pastors, as part of their role, look for the broader meaning in the events around them. They also have a front row seat for the most dramatic moments in the lives of the people they serve. As a result, a fair number of pastors have the hidden or visible desire to write, to share the wisdom they have gained. It may be as simple as sharing the advice they wish they'd given a troubled teen years ago, or as subtle as the beauty of the graceful death of a person of great faith. Many of us have stories to tell, and many of us have the dream that "someday" we'll be able to set aside the time to tell them. For those who have always wanted time to write, being the pastor of a small church can be the sabbatical that makes it possible.

You may find that the appeal of becoming the pastor of a small church is the way you can provide some basic support for your life and use part of your time to pursue something you have always dreamed of doing. If you are in a stage of life where this is possible and it appeals to you, the mix of having fun while doing good can make for a quite satisfying pattern of life.

QUESTIONS FOR REFLECTION AND DISCUSSION

1. How does your church cope with financial stresses?
2. What has brought you through the lean times?
3. Does the burden of worrying about money fall on the pastor?

18

Small Churches Are Worth Loving

IS THERE A PLACE FOR THE SMALL CHURCH?

SOME FOLKS SEEM TO think that the small church is a dying breed that should just be put out of its misery. It can be much more exciting to look at the emerging church, the multicultural church, the church without walls, or any of the many free and exhilarating new ways to live out our spiritual lives. Small-church people can seem boring, behind the times, and resistant to change. There is a sense from some that small-church people should simply get out of the way, sell the buildings, and let the church be transformed into something completely different.

I disagree. I believe that the hope of the future for our mainline denominations lies in the small churches. What our small churches need is not abandonment to despair, but a reforming and revival based on the gospel we share. The small church is the place where revival can happen—where prayer happens, where Scripture is heard and adopted, where the Holy Spirit works in individual lives, and where people help each other grow as disciples of Jesus.

The small church is not, and never will be, more entertaining than the movies or more fun than hanging out at the club, but it can be far more joyful. It can fill the hunger in a heart for significance, meaning, and a caring family of brothers and sisters. In spite of our individual sinfulness, we know that this is really possible as long as the church is grounded in the gospel of Christ, guided by the Spirit, and sincerely trying to live together as Christians.

The small church is a place where people can become disciples, encourage each other, and work at the process of growing into the image of Christ. In the hostile environment of our modern culture, the small church is the best place we have to grow into mature Christians. If you want to be part of this work of the kingdom of God, the small church is the place to find it.

SMALL CHURCHES ADDRESS OUR CULTURE'S GREATEST WEAKNESS.

One of the biggest challenges we face in our fast-moving modern culture is maintaining connections with others. Social isolation—the lack of others to talk with, relate to, or share with—has become pervasive. Even though we may be connected through email, voice mail, text messaging, or "social" websites, these mediated communications do not provide the depth and emotional connection of direct personal contact. The results of an important study on social isolation were published in the *American Sociological Review* in June 2006. It showed significant decline in personal relationships between 1985 and 2004.[1]

Whom do you go to when you have something important and personal that you need to talk about? How many people would you feel comfortable reaching out to? These people are known as your core network of confidants: the number of people that you can confide in. This is how the study measured our connectedness to others.

The study showed that the number of confidants that the average person has declined over the twenty-year period studied, and that an increasing number of people have no one at all with whom they feel comfortable sharing a confidence. The percentage of the population who had no confidants went from 10 percent in 1985 to almost 25 percent in 2004. The average number of confidants for all people went from almost three in 1985 to nearly two in 2004. The percentage of the population with two or fewer friends went up, and the percentage of the population with three or more friends went down.

The small church is a place that works against this trend. When you are in a small church on Sunday morning, there may not be a crowd of people there, but each individual present is a brother or sister in Christ. Because the people of a small church are so deeply connected to each other, your pool of potential confidants is much larger than if you were depending on casual friends, passing neighbors, and current coworkers.

---

1. McPherson, "Social Isolation in America."

In a small church, you are surrounded by others you have or will come to know well—others who share your basic, underlying values. You are surrounded by others who are committed to helping you, just as you are committed to helping them, simply because you are all followers of Jesus together. I remember once being in a difficult place and needing someone to talk with. I took out my church directory, and I found almost thirty people I would feel comfortable calling and asking to get together to have coffee. Members of a church family are there for each other, and I was amazed to find that there were so many people I could count on to care.

As the modern culture divides us and separates us from each other, the small church remains as a place where people can find each other and build each other up in love.

WE ARE THE BODY OF CHRIST IN OUR LITTLE CORNER.

Whether your church is on a block of city streets, between shops and plazas in the suburbs, or by the side of a country road, your small church is the body of Christ in its own neighborhood. You are the ones who visibly represent Jesus to those around you, and it is from seeing you and hearing you and knowing you that your neighborhood can see what it means to follow him.

We are all meant to be living examples of the way of life Jesus taught. This means that we need to live out the gospel in all our relationships, whether they are with those closest to us in our families or with strangers we meet on our daily rounds. We are the representatives of the kingdom of God to those around us. If the kingdom of God is going to touch our neighbors, it will be with our hands and voices and hearts.

We are the ones who get to do the work of Christ in our community and through our own personal connections. If God's love is going to be expressed to those in trouble or in need, it will be we who express it. We are the ones on the front lines, the ones who recognize needs because we see them happen. We know who is living through a serious illness, who has suffered a loss, who has had a financial setback, and whose family relationships are at risk. We know when there is a need for help, because it happens right where we live.

We are also the ones who speak the gospel message into our environment. We may not use fancy words, but we are the ones to tell what it means to us to feel God's love and forgiving acceptance. We can say from our own experience what it means to be part of God's family, one of the brothers and sisters of Jesus, and included in a supportive circle of others. We are the ones who get to share the good news, one friend at a time.

We in the small church are on the front lines of doing the work of Jesus, doing it the way he did it, one person at a time. While we are doing that work, we have company in our church family, growing in faith and discipleship with each other. The beauty of growing as disciples together is that we all take turns—leading and learning, supporting and being supported, helping and being helped.

Because we are small and deeply connected to each other, the work of becoming and being Christian is one we have the chance to practice with each other every day. This is a blessing that a small church is uniquely able to provide. Small churches are definitely worth loving and worth nurturing, to continue to provide this opportunity to those who are working to grow into the image of Christ.

WE SHOULD KEEP OUR CHURCHES IN PRAYER.

Our ministries and our churches only succeed by the grace and with the help of the God we serve. Praying for our own churches and other small churches is part of our ministry. Please join me in my prayer for you:

> Lord our God,
>
> Please be within and among the people of your church, filling us with your Holy Spirit and empowering us to do your work in the world.
>
> Help us to do your work your way, from the heart, loving you and each other, and loving all those we serve, so that all will know that we belong to Christ.
>
> Be with us in our struggle to live the gospel we believe: to forgive and to live together, to grow in faith and encourage the growth of others, and to invite those who don't know you into your family.
>
> Help us to be the body of Christ in the world, whether we are few or many, listening to hear your voice and doing what you ask of us as best we can.
>
> In all things, give us strength for the journey, companions on the way, and joy in the hope of coming together one day in your house.
>
> We ask this in the name of Jesus the Christ. Amen.

So be it, Lord.

QUESTIONS FOR REFLECTION AND DISCUSSION

1. What do you love about your church?
2. What do you find difficult to love?
3. What hope do you see for small churches?
4. How can small-church people use their challenges to grow as Christians?

Bibliography

Bliese, Richard H. "Life on the edge: a small church redefines its mission." *Christian Century* 120, no 14 (2003), 24–27.

Bonhoeffer, Dietrich. *The Cost of Discipleship*. New York: Simon & Schuster, 1959.

Clark, Linda J., et al. *How We Seek God Together: Exploring Worship Style*. Bethesda, MD: Alban Institute, 2001.

————. *How We Seek God Together: Exploring Worship Style*, VHS video. Bethesda, MD: Alban Institute, 2001.

McIntosh, Gary. *One Size Doesn't Fit All: Bringing Out the Best in Any Size Church*. Grand Rapids: F.H. Revell, 1999.

McPherson, Miller, et al. "Social Isolation in America: Changes in Core Discussion Networks over Two Decades." *American Sociological Review* 71 (2006) 353–375.

Pappas, Anthony. *Entering the World of the Small Church*. Bethesda, MD: Alban Institute, 2000.

Research Services Presbyterian Church (U.S.A.), *Comparative Statistics*. Online: http://www.pcusa.org/research/compstats/index.htm.

Risley, Jean F. *Third Century and Counting, The History and Heritage of the Scotchtown Presbyterian Church.* Privately published history of the Scotchtown Presbyterian Church, Middletown, NY, 2004.

Schaller, Lyle E. *The Small Membership Church*. Nashville: Abingdon, 1994.

Tey, Josephine. *Brat Farrar*. New York: Scribner, 1997.

Tillapaugh, Frank R. *Unleashing the Church: Getting People Out of the Fortress and Into Ministry*. Ventura, CA: Regal, 1982.